On Your Bike

On Your Bike

Reflections of a Pedal Pilgrim
JOHN B THOMSON

DARTON·LONGMAN+TODD

To Graham Pigott
Spiritual Guide
and Friend.

First published in 2024 by
Darton, Longman and Todd Ltd
Unit 1, The Exchange
6 Scarbrook Road
Croydon CR0 1UH

© 2024 John B. Thomson

The right of John B. Thomson to be identified as the Author of this work has been asserted in accordance with the Copyright, Designs and Patents Act 1988.

ISBN: 978-1-913657-90-1

A catalogue record for this book is available from the British Library.

Printed and bound in Great Britain by Bell & Bain, Glasgow

Contents

Preface 7

Chapter 1	In the Saddle	13
Chapter 2	In Formation	21
Chapter 3	In Ministry	35
Chapter 4	In Suffering	49
Chapter 5	In Company	59
Chapter 6	In the Lead	73
Chapter 7	In the Spirit	86
Chapter 8	In the Rough	104
Chapter 9	In Public	126
Chapter 10	In Conclusion	144

Select Bibliography 147
Notes 159

Preface

As an enthusiastic recreational cyclist I have frequently found myself mulling over matters of discipleship and ministry whilst pedalling through the Yorkshire countryside. In the process I have come to recognise many connections between them. For example discipleship and ministry, like cycling, seek to encourage forms of life that respect creation and contest the abuses which the climate emergency has exposed. Their prophetic role reminds us that we need to tread gently upon the earth and be earthed in a materially spiritual way. Discipleship and ministry, like cycling, at their best are inclusive, catholic and hospitable to people of all ages and backgrounds. They bind people together as companions, whether as members of a cycling club or as a Church community, and thereby enable strangers to become friends. They show us the importance of agility, adaptability and flexibility in an unfolding, complex and changing reality. They involve faith, adventure, exploration, beauty, struggle, sacrifice, improvisation, apprenticeship, companionship, suffering, flexibility and the development of practical wisdom. Discipleship and ministry, like cycling, are public activities with a common interest in healthy political and civic life in order that society and indeed the Church may flourish in peace. They represent an economics of blessing, celebrating life as a gift to be received with contemplative thanks

ON YOUR BIKE

rather than a possession to be grasped by right. Yet their vulnerability in today's world also helps us to face our own vulnerability which is often experienced as suffering. Long distance cycle rides, like the marathon of discipleship and ministry, give time to reflect deeply about difficult issues of life and faith which have no simple solutions. In a world besotted by speed, such contemplative travel deepens and expands wisdom for life.

- *Chapter 1* explores discipleship and ministry through the eye of a cyclist.
- *Chapter 2* shows that we best learn about cycling, discipleship and ministry through challenging practice. Reflecting on ministerial formation in South Africa during the latter years of apartheid I show how we learn most, as Jesus taught us, through the gift of strangers.
- *Chapter 3* draws upon thirty years of ministry in Yorkshire to argue that fruitful and effective ministry requires that we give significant time to learn the history, stories and language of the people and the places we serve. Like cycling a regular route this is about discovering the richness and variety of the landscape and its communities who teach us how to speak the faith in a way faithful to Pentecost.
- *Chapter 4* uses my experience of being taken ill whilst out cycling to explore the nature and character of suffering, which is often seen as a major challenge for discipleship and ministry. I argue that we can live creatively and hopefully, even in tragedy, in the light of the story of Jesus.
- *Chapter 5* argues that following and serving Christ, like cycling, is a social rather than a singular experience. It unpacks the social and theological meaning of the Church for disciples and ministers of Christ.

PREFACE

- *Chapter 6* explores a number of key themes of Christian leadership concluding that the majority of Christian leaders, like those who lead cycle rides, are relatively unknown but actually have the most impact on others.
- *Chapter 7* argues that cycling, discipleship and ministry involve the body. Spirituality is therefore material and for this world rather than an escape into something otherworldly. I explore what this looks like through the lenses of sight, sound, sight and sign.
- *Chapter 8* recognises that discipleship and ministry, like cycling, bring challenges which are not always easy to resolve. In this chapter I use three case studies to explore three such challenging issues. The first is about the place of truth in liberal societies, the second is about sexuality and the third is about climate change and fracking.
- *Chapter 9* notes that cycling, discipleship and ministry are public activities with important insights for society in areas such as volunteering, sovereignty, politics, the good life, economics and law.
- *Chapter 10* summarises the arguments made in earlier chapters.

I have had many companions on this journey. I am particularly indebted to Graham Pigott, whose wise counsel has guided me over the past twenty years and whose wisdom infuses much of what is written here. I am also grateful to Stephen Cottrell, Helen Williams and Philip Lewis who read early drafts and made helpful comments which have improved the text and to David Moloney of Darton, Longman and Todd who kept faith with the project despite the challenges of COVID and its legacy. The faith of my parents and of African Christians inspired me at an early age. They lived an adventure which was compelling and challenging. Christians in local churches, universities, seminaries and other walks of life have helped me discover and explore the richness of ministry. In particular my wife Sue has exhibited a humble, committed yet diffident discipleship whilst our daughters, Anya and Emily along with son-in-law Jonny and grandchildren Alice and Barnaby, challenge me to live in a way that embodies the story I am part of. I am also indebted to Stanley Hauerwas, whose work has helped me wrestle with discipleship and ministry for over three decades.[1]

ACKNOWLEDGEMENTS

I am grateful to Hymns Ancient & Modern for permission to use John B. Thomson, *Living Holiness: Stanley Hauerwas And The Church* (Epworth: London, 2010), pp.88–91 in Chapter 3 and to Sacristy Limited for permission to use Gavin Wakefield and Nigel Rooms, *Northern Gospel, Northern Church: Reflections on Identity and Mission* (Durham Sacristy Press, 2016), pp. 93-95.

NOTES

First the racial descriptions used in this book reflect those I encountered in South Africa at the time. Whilst recent visits to South Africa suggest that most continue to be used, I am aware that some may find them anachronistic. However since I am drawing upon memories from the time, I have decided to express them in ways that reflect how they appeared to me then. I apologise if this causes any offence.

Secondly, this book was mainly written before the COVID pandemic. However its intended publication date was delayed by the legacy of COVID and so whilst I have made reference to it as I have revised the original

PREFACE

text I have not given it a separate chapter. Nevertheless Chapter 4 does offer an analogous reflection on suffering and struggle which has some cross over with the impact of COVID.

CHAPTER 1
In the Saddle

BIKING IN BARE FEET

Uganda in the 1960s was a land of bikes and bare feet. Cars were around, but only for the relatively affluent and for taxi drivers. The former were a minority and the latter a nightmare. I recall being overtaken by an overloaded Peugeot 404 Estate car on the road from Kampala to Entebbe. As it roared past us well above the legal speed limit I noticed that it looked familiar. In fact it was our former car written off some months earlier when a rogue driver had crashed into my father on the road out of Kampala to Masaka to the southeast of the capital. What had been declared a wreck was now careering along risking the lives of the twelve people crammed into it like tinned sardines. At least the sort of bikes prevalent on roads were sturdy roadsters, which travel at a slower speed, often overloaded with people or goods. Matoke, the staple plantain in the local diet, was piled high on these bikes, as were furniture, animals and just about anything else. In Uganda travelling by bike was normal and accessible for all ages and this sense of normality explains why I have remained a cyclist since my childhood. Furthermore cycling beats foot and car for most journeys under 10kms. It also has good green credentials and health benefits. Yet not all those I've worked with have shared this view. My first major conflict with my training vicar was about cycling and the luminous socks I wore. In his view my being a redhead was one thing. Arriving for visits with a red face and wearing luminous pink or green socks was too much. Nevertheless, I held out and the bike and the socks won!

BIKING AND PASSION

Cycling though is not simply about utility and practicality. It represents a passion for those of us who love it just as faith involves passion for God. Passion for God directs how we travel through life, guides the choices we make, informs the messages we share, sustains us in the struggles we wrestle with and clarifies the priorities we hold to. In particular, passion for God gives life a goal, which is to embrace, celebrate and exhibit the generous love of God expressed in the self-giving, sacrificial story of Jesus Christ. A decade or so ago I learned the meaning of passion when I entered the Cycle Touring Club's Phil Liggett Challenge Ride in Derbyshire.[1] Cyclists ranging from Lycra-clad Audax enthusiasts to recreational week-enders took part in this ride of 100 or 150 kilometres through some of the most stunning, beautiful and challenging countryside in England, including climbs up Holme Moss, Winnats Pass, and Monsall Head. At the time I was commuting several times a week by bike between our home in Doncaster and my office in Rotherham and so was reasonably fit. However, not having done such a challenging ride, I cautiously opted for the 100 kilometre route. At the outset of the ride I teamed up with another rider who challenged me when we got to the halfway mark to complete the 150 kilometre ride. Enthusiasm got the better of me and so I agreed. The climb up Winnats Pass exposed my limitations and not long afterwards I learned the double meaning of passion when I rounded a sharp corner, hit some gravel on the road, came off the bike suffering cuts and bruises and ruptured the front tyre. As a result I had to withdraw from the ride and phone my wife to ask her to drive from Doncaster to Baslow in Derbyshire to pick me up since my car was in Stannington, in west Sheffield over 25 kilometres away.

Passion is a key word in the Christian lexicon and is at the heart of good ministry. It describes the suffering love of Christ for us and what it means for us to love Christ. Christians are therefore passion people since the love of Christ has captivated us. This is at the heart of any calling to ministry. Passion can feel like the endorphin kick of a great ride or the exhilaration of cycling through wonderful landscapes. Yet passion brings suffering. Like a long cycle ride ministry tests us to our limits and exposes whether we really love all aspects of this journey or are simply fair weather riders. When the weather turns against us or the hill climb causes our lungs to burst and our tired legs to scream we find ourselves praying passionately in what feels like the dark night of the soul. Yet this suffering forms us to become stronger and we see our calling more clearly just as through his struggles St. Paul discovered how much he loved Jesus Christ.

BIKING AND FAITH

Cycling also gives us time to reflect on faith. For example Baptism literally means a soaking and cyclists are regularly soaked when riding in the rain. Pilgrimage is a prayerful journey with God and many times cyclists can be heard praying 'Oh my God!' on a challenging ride. Holy communion is where our spiritual hunger is fed with the life of Jesus just as a stretching bike ride builds up an appetite which can only be satisfied with a good meal. Fellowship means a practical sharing of life and resources and cyclists display fellowship when they respond to a rider with a puncture or a broken chain. One of the Greek words for salvation can also mean health and cycling is one of the healthiest and cheapest forms of exercise in God's gym, the great outdoors. Cycling has its celebrity saints such as Bradley Wiggins, Lizzie

ON YOUR BIKE

Armistead, Chris Froome, or Lizzie Deignan who show us how to cycle well even if we can't match them. And just as the Bible is a library of stories so the cycling community is awash with anecdotes and stories of adventures and challenges, highlights and lowlights which are full of morals and guidance for other cyclists. Furthermore cycling fosters community since it is a sport for all ages and genders. It cultivates face to face relationships, respects creation, has a low carbon footprint, improves health, keeps bank accounts healthier and forms friendships.

As an enthusiastic cyclist I encourage as many people as are able to cycle. Indeed younger clergy and lay ministers in most circumstances are better cycling around their parishes than arriving in a car as a sort of emergency service. Cycling in urban areas and even in rural ones is often as quick as the car, gives time for reflection between appointments and makes one accessible in a way that the glass of a car windscreen and windows prohibits. Cycling also has health and financial benefits. When I was a vicar my travel expenses were less than the standard travel fee paid by the undertakers because I cycled to the crematorium and back. Cycling can also get one out of trouble. Once I received a phone call at 10.25 a.m. from an undertaker asking where I was. I said that I was expecting to be with him for an 11.00 a.m. service and that my wife was due back with the car in ten minutes. 'But the service is due at 10.30 a.m.' he said! I had our toddler daughter with me so I raced next door to a neighbour, left our child with her, grabbed my panniers, packed my robes, got on the bike and cycled at full pelt for over two miles to the crematorium. I arrived at around 10.45am and took the service somewhat red faced and after profuse apologies to the family. Thankfully the number of mourners was modest and the service simple so we finished two minutes before the next funeral. The bike was indeed good news that morning. The good news we share as ministers of the Gospel is that we are all invited to ride with passion on life's open road with God. Even when things surprise us or we slip up, as I did with those funeral arrangements, or even fall off, as I did on the Phil Liggett ride, we discover that God's love embodied in Jesus never lets us down or leaves us. This wonderful reality not only energises us but frames our faith journey and points to its destiny. That's why my enthusiasm for the good news of cycling is only exceeded by my enthusiasm for the good news of Christ.

BIKING AND CHARACTER

Cycling for long periods of time develops character. It slows one down, tests perseverance and deepens contemplation. Depth and perseverance are difficult to achieve in a fast moving, technologically driven, choice laden society. The opportunity costs of sticking with something for the long haul are always nagging at us as we see other attractions and opportunities around us. Yet the wisdom tradition of the Bible, particularly seen in Job and Proverbs shows that formation of character takes time and pain if it is to be transformative. This is also clear from the shape of Jesus' life as he spent thirty years preparing for his ministry and three years actively engaged in it, culminating in the three days we call the Passion.

In my own ministry certain experiences have been transformative. For example, when in 1989 I was appointed as a tutor at St Paul's College Grahamstown in South Africa, now called Makhanda, the challenge to my identity as a white, western Christian was a surprise and shock. Even as a public minister of the Church I found myself representing 400 years of white history in South Africa. I was told that western theology was pietistic and paid little attention to the social and political implications of key biblical stories such as the Exodus. I was exposed to

ON YOUR BIKE

a way of doing theology which saw me, a white person, as part of the oppression experienced by the black majority.[2] So preparing ordinands for ministry in this environment was very challenging, especially as I was working within a different church tradition to my own. This radical and social Anglo-Catholicism left me wondering whether my own spiritual journey was indeed pious escapism. I had long conversations about it with my Spiritual Director who helped me reflect upon these challenges in a way that reshaped my vision of ministry, my identity as a white person and my understanding of the Church. As a consequence when we returned to England I accepted the post of vicar in inner urban Doncaster in the North of England, a context quite unlike anything I had met before.

A second transformative experience happened while I was Director of Ministry in the Diocese of Sheffield. I had loved parish ministry in Doncaster and with a PhD in ecclesiology I felt that I was equipped to help lead the ministerial training and development department in the Diocese. Yet this role was perplexing. It was difficult to gain any momentum and I found parish clergy were sceptical about training and development and instead were caught up in the immediate demands of their own parishes. As a vicar I had a good-sized congregation with enthusiastic though not always confident leaders; I now led a team of specialists but had no congregation. Diocesan training events were precarious and attendance was lower than equivalent parish events. As a result I became anxious about my performance. I felt I was sinking and drowning without a clear sense of what I could do about it. God seemed even further away than when I was a curate and vicar. I felt that God was absent and wondered if I had mistaken God's calling.

It was during my second year in the role that I was put in touch with a new Spiritual Director who helped me to mine this dark experience for its treasures. I slowly found that I was able to hallow and host my struggles. I stopped trying to control outcomes or justify myself and instead sought to hear God's loving call in my fragility. I discovered a deeper trust as I asked, 'Who is God for me and who am I for God?' As I wrestled with challenges to my identity, integrity, reputation and competence as a minister I found myself being re-formed. I discovered the wisdom of the fourth century desert ascetics with their challenge to stay in my cell and it would teach me everything. I came to see that the drive to seek another ministry was a form of escapism and a lack of trust in God's providence. I would simply be fleeing as an unrefined self, unwilling to trust God for the future. Instead I needed to become faithful, focussed and forgiving so that I could move from being driven to receptivity and discover in these testing times that God was authoring me in a strange yet profound way, showing me that my vocation was where my pain was. Like Christ in Mark 1:12 I felt as if I had been kicked into a desert. Yet God turned this desert into a dessert of blessing as ministry became deeper, richer and more trusting. I found myself digging deeper rather than fleeing, staying with challenges rather than ducking them and walking into struggle rather than running away from it.

CONCLUSION

Faith and ministry, like cycling, take us on a journey through the fierce landscape of life serving a challenging, mysterious and yet loving God who invites us to become contemplative and brooding, waiting and watching for the One who is never in a hurry. If we are to grow extensively we must first grow intensively and discover in the constraints, struggles and challenges of life opportunities to learn and trust that God's future will come to meet us. We have to relinquish our self-projected goals and dreams, which we easily confuse with God's will, and let God be the horizon of our lives if we are to have space for God. And as God de-centres us we find that

ON YOUR BIKE

we can embrace working incognito like God as we see that Jerusalem, where a suffering, dying Jesus asks God why He has forsaken him, is actually more important in the story of salvation than Galilee where Jesus seems to be successful as a religious leader.[3]

Questions for reflection

1. How does your passion as a Christian show itself?
2. What aspect of cycling most clearly illuminates your faith?
3. In what way has cycling enriched your faith and ministry?
4. What has been the most transformative moment in your faith and ministry?

CHAPTER 2
In Formation

TRIKE TO BIKE

My first memories of riding a bike were when I was about three and I was given a green tricycle for my birthday. We were living in Uganda at the time, and since Uganda is on the Equator and the weather is warm, pedalling was possible throughout the year even during the rainy season. The tyres were solid rather than inflatable so, though uncomfortable, there were never any punctures and with a bit of practice and bravado, doing cycle tricks became the norm. Nevertheless this was nursery cycling and when at the age of six and I was given a bicycle I had to perfect the art of staying upright before I could test the bike's possibilities. I can still remember seeing how long I could stay on the bike as I pedalled along a dirt track at the bottom of our garden. Slowly I gained confidence and then it was full steam ahead with other children as we cycled all over the university campus, jumping the speed humps with alacrity and putting cardboard in our wheels so that we could make as much noise as we could. The bike gave us relative freedom in this safe space, though once to the consternation of my mother I was taken, riding pillion, by a Ugandan friend into the local slum area. On another occasion a couple of local lads managed to persuade me to 'lend' them my bike by passing it to them though a

ON YOUR BIKE

gap in the university campus fence. Hearing of this act of generosity my mother jumped into the car with us, drove rapidly to where the lads were and swiftly recovered the bike from the suitably penitent thieves! It taught me a lesson. Whilst learning to cycle freed me for adventure it also brought risks as it opened up a strange and more complex world.

STRANGER FORMATION

One of the noticeable features of the teaching of Jesus is his focus on loving strangers. To love those who are very different from ourselves is to learn the real challenge of love since we are not relating to another person for any other reason than love. This is particularly the case with those most estranged to us, those who we perceive to be our enemies. It is also the meaning of the New Testament Greek word for hospitality, *philoxenia*.[1] Such love echoes the character of divine love which sends rain upon the just and the unjust.[2] To love strangers opens us up to learning from them, an education which is often much more demanding and formative than remaining with those we like and feel are like us. This sort of education is particularly important in ministerial formation since ministry involves expressing the love of God who seeks the wellbeing of strangers and enemies.

A STRANGE COUNTY

In 1984 I was given the opportunity to spend the best part of a year in the company of very challenging strangers. They exposed me to a richer and more expansive vision of the Christian faith and of ministry than I had encountered before and disturbed and challenged many of my settled convictions about faith and ministry. While I was training for ordination I had developed a friendship with a South African priest who encouraged me to arrange a student exchange between our two Theological Colleges: St Paul's College, Grahamstown (now known as Makhanda), South Africa and Wycliffe Hall, Oxford.[3] In August 1984 I went to St Paul's for two academic terms and was plunged into a society in crisis with the Anglican Church at the forefront of confrontation with the apartheid regime. My Ugandan childhood had equipped me to feel at home in African cultures, but I was not prepared for the naked racism which I met in the South Africa. My parents had ensured that we were brought up among people of all ethnicities, and in the Ugandan Church ebony and ivory broadly prayed in harmony. In South Africa however, ebony and ivory struggled in agony.

A STRANGE SOCIETY

At that time South Africa was governed by the Group Areas Act, which determined where a person could live based upon the colour of their skin and so the commitment of the College to be non-racial was not only illegal but also offered a unique experiment in social living for its South African students. This social living involved major adjustments for many students. A number of black students told me that they could not sleep when they first arrived at the College because the area was so quiet. Their homes were in very noisy townships and so they felt at home in this environment. The quiet of the College was unnerving. Gradually they would adjust to the quiet, but then when they returned home found that they could not sleep because they now found the noise intrusive.

White students also faced difficult issues at this time. One sensitive issue was white conscription into the military since black students saw resistance to this as a test of white commitment to the anti-apartheid struggle. The upshot was some very heated College meetings

ON YOUR BIKE

at which different perspectives and pressures tested the community's common life to the full. Black students were familiar with suffering as part of their resistance to apartheid. White students struggled with the costs involved in resisting the state especially as it could result in imprisonment.

Another sensitive issue was the relationship between theology and violence. In a context where there was no democratic way of changing society some students felt that the Just War Theory gave violence legitimacy in South Africa. Attending a treason trial in Grahamstown with fellow students brought home to all of us the implications of such theology and its attendant risks. Yet these heated debates showed the depth of their commitment to a ministry of integrity in a Christian community damaged by the legacy of apartheid and thereby challenged my more pietistic and individualistic spirituality. At Oxford, faith was seen primarily as an individualistic relationship with Christ. The Church was a support rather than an essential element of this relationship. In South Africa, spirituality was social and political and the Church was essential.

A STRANGE ECONOMICS

In Grahamstown poverty was everywhere with children and adults begging openly on the street. The contrast between predominantly black poverty and white affluence was sharp in a town full of private fee paying schools and a University. Grahamstown Area Distress Relief Association (GADRA) established in 1958 sought to respond to this poverty. For more than 30 years the organisation's primary activities were geared towards aiding the poor and marginalised, including people with disabilities. I signed up with them to help in a soup kitchen as part of a social action project called Open Doors. They offered soup and bread at a cost of ten cents and a warm

IN FORMATION

meal cost a rand. It was humbling and fascinating to talk with clients about the realities of life for them under apartheid. With the need to survive on limited income and minimal opportunities for education and employment, the majority community was excluded from accessing any real power to affect change. Only in education, health care and religious communities were there leadership opportunities for those in the black community. Yet even under such oppression they did not reject God, but rather prayed and worked for a better future. For them, Church, faith and dignity were at the heart of the struggle against apartheid.

A STRANGE HISTORY

The apartheid system was crucial to maintaining poverty which was why the poor were hidden away in townships or Bantustans. Colonialism was also a contributor to black poverty in particular and fellow students were very critical of the legacy of Britain in South Africa. Although I had studied South African History as part of my degree at York and was aware of the story of South Africa I found this deep ambivalence towards Britain a shock. As a child I was vaguely aware that certain groups in Uganda, particularly in the Kingdom of Buganda who were the largest tribe, shared these reservations. For example, when the Kabaka, the local king of Buganda, died in 1969 whilst in exile in England, rumours abounded that he had been poisoned by the British. As a result, we had to leave Kampala whilst the funeral took place for our own safety. I recall how the generosity of my visiting elderly grandfather got us through military roadblocks when he offered Pontefract Cakes to bullet-belted soldiers. Such outbursts against white people, though, were few. By contrast in South Africa the critique was more outright especially of the liberal tradition with its formal, though not often effective, commitment to the equal dignity of all people. Hypocrisy and double standards were challenged and a white skin represented privilege regardless of whether one was critical of apartheid. Even groups, such as the feminist Black Sash movement, were regarded by many in the black community as affluent whites who could not identify with their experience and struggle. Ironically a number of black students told me that they had more respect for racist Afrikaaners than for English speaking liberals since at least they knew where they stood with them. I therefore found myself a prisoner of this sharply criticised history rather than a representative of a constructive tradition. It made me much more aware of how situated we are, how we are involuntary signs of our social history and how we can only be with but not become part of those communities which have a very different experience of that history and tradition.

This reaction against white history and its legacy also meant that there was a great deal of criticism of western theology in the College which was seen as serving the interests of white domination. Many students also regarded their academic work as less significant than their active fight against the apartheid system and their support of the destitute. Giving primacy to action and transformation also raised questions about the nature of theology. Was theology a set of abstract ideas about God and the world that we try to put into practice, or did theology emerge through the practices and performance of the Christian life? In Oxford the assumption was that practice flowed from theological theory. Application was for the individual or a subgroup to work out. In South Africa practice generated questions about God's ways with the world which then challenged the Christian community to reflect deeply about the nature of God's call in their setting.

IN FORMATION

A STRANGE SPIRITUALITY

African spirituality infused College life, ensuring that ministry could have a surprising shape as I discovered when a student called Sizwe unexpectedly began to exhibit health problems. He was diagnosed with a blood clot, but although this was dealt with, he still remained unwell and withdrawn. Yet when I visited him in his hospital bed, his grip was very strong and his eyes were aflame. The puzzle became clearer when we learned that someone back in Zululand had cast a spell on him. The College Principal, Duncan Buchanan, arranged for an exorcism and thereafter Sizwe's health swiftly improved and he returned to the College. I found this episode very puzzling. Did such spells induce autosuggestion manifested as illness, or was this evil in action? How did this fit into the other theology we were learning? How was such African theology shaping my own ministerial development as I was exposed to heated debates about the veneration of ancestors, traditional rites of passage like male circumcision, the place of traditional medicine and customs around death? What sense could I make of the charismatic revival among white and coloured students? Was this an escape from the realities of apartheid by retreating into a 'spiritual sphere' of personal encounter with God, or was it a refreshing renewing of stale spirituality in order to face apartheid's impacts with confidence and hope? For example, one white ordinand told me that his charismatic encounter with Christ and the impact of black people's stories of suffering caused him to break down and weep in the chapel as he heard about their pain for the first time. I found such stories inverting standard views of power and transformation as the suffering community exposed the emptiness of affluence, spoke of the need to side with the poor and re-narrated Christian history from the perspective of the marginalised. Abe Jacobs, one of the more vocal of these ordinands, asserted that 'the rich are poor' and used the Confessing Church in Germany led by Dietrich

ON YOUR BIKE

Bonhoeffer as a model of the sort of Church needed in an apartheid society. The Confessing Church believed that most of the German Churches had capitulated to Hitler and the Nazis. They refused to see Hitler as the Ruler of the Church and expressed their convictions in the Barmen Declaration (1934). They held that only Christ could be the Head of the Church and this led them to resist Hitler, resistance, which eventually led to Bonhoeffer's execution following a failed assassination attempt on Hitler. For Abe the Church had to stand against apartheid just as Bonhoeffer and the Confessing Church had stood against Hitler.

A STRANGE EXPERIENCE

Life in South Africa was stressful therefore, yet it was also renewing and on occasions comic. For example, when I visited the Ciskei as part of a College placement I experienced hospitality, smiles, communal living and worship reflecting the generosity of African culture.[4] I also met the local priest who refused to learn to drive so that he wouldn't have to spend his life in a car visiting all the many chapelries in his parish. Instead on Saturday evenings he would lead a service in his house and consecrate enough Holy Communion for catechists to take to the chapelries the next day. In contrast on a mission in the Transkei our team joined the parish priest, Madoda Hlwathika, and his catechists as they visited homes in the villages to pray with people. As we left each house those we had prayed for joined us and within an hour there was a long line of people snaking their way across the countryside going from house to house.

Less comic was the visit of a neighbouring white cleric who came to ask Madoda why we were not involved in his parish as well. I had actually refused to work with him because it was said that he had shot a parishioner in the foot during an argument and I didn't feel that this would bode well for mission in his parishes. The altercation with Madoda was lively and since I was trying to sleep in the room next door I could hear the argument getting progressively more aggressive, fuelled by a drunk colleague of the visiting cleric. Thankfully both the cleric and his friend eventually departed without any violence, but it felt surreal! Equally surreal was Madoda's Christmas bonus. This was a huge pig which ate everything left around the place and snored noisily, separated from me only by a brick wall. Tragically Madoda was killed in a road accident after I had left South Africa. This was a common occurrence in the Transkei since many had had no proper driving lessons or roadworthy vehicles and roads were potholed, often dirt roads rather than tarmac.

A STRANGE CHURCH

One of the more surprising features of the Church in these rural settings was that it was sustained by its laity. It was surprising because the tradition of the Church was Anglo-Catholic with its historic emphasis upon ordained ministry. Yet in every parish the Mothers' Union and the lay catechists were the backbone of the ministry of the local church. Madoda had 19 chapel outstations and so could only visit each one every three months for baptisms, Eucharist and administration. He therefore depended on catechists and Mothers' Union members to sustain the Church's ministry and mission in his absence. This reality also shaped the debate about the ordination of women to the priesthood. During a Diocesan Synod in Grahamstown an elderly Xhosa man stood up and said 'in our community when a man dies nothing changes. When a woman dies everything collapses. Therefore women should be ordained!'

ON YOUR BIKE

REFLECTIONS ON THE GIFT OF STRANGERS
Social faith

This time in South Africa formed my faith and ministry in ways I would not have imagined if I had remained back in England. First, I became much more aware of the social character of discipleship and the significance of the Church. The Xhosa phrase *umtu ngabuntu ngabantu* which means a person is a person because of other persons reflects an African anthropology which is closer to the thinking of the biblical era than contemporary western individualism. This could be adapted to 'a disciple is a disciple because of other disciples'. Ministry therefore involves cultivating Christian communities as witnesses of the Gospel so that they are formed to see God's action in the world. Christian communities therefore read Scripture, practise liturgy and explore theology in public with others as interpreting communities who thereby better discern God's ways in life. And this formation includes the insights of the global and historic Church to ensure that local understanding is not culturally captive. For Anglicans this involves contextualisation and contest within a social Catholicism that has been and is developed at its grass roots.[5]

Power and faith

Secondly, I became much more sensitive to the place of power in life, faith and ministry. Abusive power was endemic in apartheid South Africa and the majority community were excluded from quality education, jobs and prospects because power was in the hands of the white minority. Poverty was also about powerlessness, poverty which brought suffering to the majority in South Africa even though traditional African communalism mitigated it. Nelson Mandela, Archbishop Tutu and other black leaders showed me that suffering can be redemptive and character building. However the abuse of power also required addressing issues of power and its abuse in order to contrast this with a vision of good power in society and Church. This was a vision of cross-shaped power, which releases rather than constrains, serves rather than dominates and reduces suffering rather than intensifying it. It is the opposite of the apartheid power since it respects human dignity, agency and binds people together rather than dividing them to rule.

Fragility and faith

Thirdly, the South African Church showed me that fragility is characteristic of faith and indeed ministry reminding us that we are not in control. The Church in South Africa was a fragile institution mainly held together by the commitment of lay people, particularly women, often in dispersed settings or challenging townships and under the pressures of apartheid. Clergy certainly mattered, but not as much as I had expected given the sacramental tradition of the Church. With limited income the Church could not finance many clergy and so local churches were led by catechists and the Mothers' Union. Together they showed me that faith is about trust in situations of vulnerability, an insight which caused me to reassess my openness to ministry in fragile communities in England.

Place and faith

Fourthly, formation among strangers clarified that mission and ministry are contextual or situated. We are always somewhere and see from a particular place rather than from a universal perspective which is only possible for God. I had some awareness of this from my parents' commitment to serving the Church in Uganda by learning local languages. Ministry after Pentecost means learning the languages of those we serve rather than expecting them to learn our language. In this way we honour their culture as we depend on local speakers to teach us how to share faith in culturally apt ways. This view of mission is in stark contrast to the standard account which frames missionaries as agents of imperialism and colonialism.[6] No doubt some were. However in Uganda I encountered missionaries who were committed to indigenous culture and leadership, to honouring local languages and to helping emerging Churches and Nations assert their distinctive identity. As a result, whilst in South Africa I tried to learn some Xhosa and Afrikaans in order to understand more about these cultures. In addition when I returned to England I saw more clearly that ministry would involve my learning the dialect and culture of the English communities I was called to serve rather than expecting them to conform to my culture and dialect.

Brokenness and faith

Fifthly, ministerial formation in South Africa faced me with the brokenness of the Church in a particularly intense way. Not only was this evident in the piety of Afrikaaners who claimed that apartheid was the will of God but it was also present in the Anglican Church as moral laxity, abusive power, gender relationships and quests for coercive power undermined this sign of grace. Yet it was clear that this brokenness did not render the Church redundant in South Africa and it was possible to see in its life together a provisional though fallible sign of God's universal society emerging in the struggle against apartheid. Ministry as is clear from St Paul's letters is about helping Christian communities to realise that God is with them even in their brokenness and that bearing one another's burdens and staying with each other even when we disagree is part of our witness to the God who works through our failings.

IN FORMATION

White and faith

My sixth point is that my time in South Africa, forced me to acknowledge that I am white. Although, as mentioned above, I was aware of the privileges of being white in Uganda, it was in South Africa that I was able to see the fuller character of white privilege, power and prejudice which was legally enforced with a vigour that put Uganda's soft racism into the shade. South Africa also taught me that white saviours, white ignorance and white inaction were no longer tolerable whether in wider society or in the Church, issues that the twenty-first-century Black Lives Matter Movement has also raised. I became aware that my whiteness, though not chosen, nevertheless gave me privileges and power simply by being white. Painfully at St Paul's College unconscious bias which regarded a white perspective as normative was robustly challenged by black students.

Culture and faith

Finally ministerial formation in another culture showed me that simple comparisons between churches across the world leads to misunderstanding. For example in much of Africa the state is dysfunctional or oppressive and politics is dangerous. Churches therefore act as communities of agency, hope and transformation much like they did in Medieval Europe. In modern Britain and much of Europe, the impact of the Peace of Westphalia of 1685, which ended the 'wars of religion', has privatised religion and marginalised it from public life. The social settings of religious understanding, practice and social involvement are therefore very different. To assume that sub Saharan Africa has the answer to western secularisation is as misguided as western Europeans assuming that they can rescue or save Africa. Ministry is about enabling Christians to become faithful witnesses in their own contexts and trusting that others in different settings are seeking to do this as well.

CONCLUSION

Ministry is about sense making, seeking to understand the ways of God in the world through the lenses of Scripture, tradition and sound learning. John V. Taylor's thinking is particularly helpful in this regard. Taylor had been formed by his experiences of ministry in Uganda and so was aware of how creative and disturbing learning from strangers can be, learning which reflects the work of the Holy Spirit as the 'and' relating us to God, to others and to the world, each of which is different to the other.[7] This 'and' Spirit enables us to see that God is primarily with us in the stranger and the ordinary rather than in the familiar and the extraordinary. And it is this strange Spirit woven into creation who challenges our sense of being in control in order to form us into a new sort of humane community, the Church, which signs that Christ is for all.

Questions for reflection

1. How do you respond to Jesus' challenge to love strangers?
2. Which strangers have most shaped your vision of faith and ministry?
3. What did you learn about faith and ministry from them?
4. In the light of this, how should the church train its disciples and ministers?

CHAPTER 3
In Ministry

MINISTRY AND LYCRA

Most cyclists have their favourite loops or circuits. As a 'middle-aged man in Lycra', or 'mamil', Doncaster and Selby have given me a range of easily accessible loops from our home. The Trans Pennine Trail is accessible from Warmsworth, a suburb of Doncaster and Barlby near Selby, so I have used it for loops which took me around the western fringes of Doncaster to places such as Cusworth Hall, Conisbrough Castle, Edlington and Wadworth, as well as round the rural villages of Selby District. Summer rides along the River Don were particularly spectacular with a viaduct framing the view. On Saturdays I would do longer rides to Wentworth Woodhouse or loop through the villages of Denaby, Thryberg, Ravenfield and back home through Edlington. As one of my clergy colleagues said this part of South Yorkshire is 'one of the undiscovered beauty spots in England'. Motorway driving misses the delights of the countryside swapping beauty and contemplation for ease and speed. Cycling gives a rider access to England in a way denied to the motor vehicle. Cycling also encourages sociability. I found that pedestrians and drivers without windscreens greeted me. Those enclosed in their vehicle didn't. Glass isolates people and is a sign of isolated individualism, whereas the bike builds community on the road. Riding regularly throughout the year also exposes one to the seasons and weather. Winter, spring, summer and autumn each have their particular character. while rain, snow and sunshine, cold and warmth all impact the rider. Like baptism this is an experience of immersion and most of the time I find it exhilarating, creative and refreshing since each season teaches one different things about cycling as well as nature. Furthermore the rhythmic and regular cadence of cycling encourages contemplation, which enables one to reflect about one's life.

MINISTRY AND PLACE

Cycling has taught me to appreciate the details and depths of a place. The first thirty-three years of my life were peripatetic and I had become an 'Anywhere' person.[1] While living in Uganda we had returned every two years to the UK until I was 12 years old. During these visits we stayed in various parts of England and Scotland as temporary visitors with all the challenges this presented at local schools. From the age of 11 until I was 16 I lived in Edinburgh while my parents were seeking a permanent situation following our departure from Uganda. Of these five years, three were spent at boarding school and two were spent living with the rest of the family in my grandmother's house in Edinburgh. Edinburgh was followed by two years at a school in North London where I studied for my A levels. Then I spent nine months in Devon assisting clergy in the parishes of Willand and Cullompton near Exeter, followed by three years reading History at York University.

After university, I returned to North London and spent a year as a care assistant at Harefield Hospital before three years' training as an ordinand at Wycliffe Hall in Oxford which included a nine-month placement in South Africa. I then had a four-year curacy in Sheffield before returning for three years and a term to South Africa as a tutor at St Paul's College in Grahamstown as described in the previous chapter. All this moving around gave me a panoramic view of life and the Church. As described in Chapter 2, South Africa also introduced me to communities very different to my own cultural background and showed me that God's love is for all people, especially for those on the margins.[2] All this was to change when we moved in 1993 to Doncaster where I became vicar of St Mary's Wheatley. All my public ministry since has been in Yorkshire and as a result I have become more of a 'Somewhere' person. Indeed, when we left Doncaster after 21 years in the town, a wisecracker quipped, 'You've been here so long, you've reached your "Sel-by" date!'

MINISTRY AND THE NORTH

Fragility is a common experience for church and society in the North of England.[3] Most congregations are fragile apart from a few middle class suburban and city-centre churches, while in economic terms much of the North continues to lament the loss of traditional industries and feels marginalized by the domination of the South-East in the service and financial sectors.[4] In political terms the North is less influential than the South-East as the difficulty of getting politicians to sort out the Railways in the North of England shows. In psychological terms significant sectors of the post-industrial North remain locked in a bereavement narrative fed by memories of an impressive but departed industrial past. In educational terms the North values practical learning given its industrial and rural heritage yet across the country Higher Education still takes the lion's share of national funding.

Much of the North represents a precariat society. According to Guy Standing, the precariat are an emerging and expansive social group characterised by economic and social insecurity at all levels and reflect the impact of globalisation on traditional forms of employment and society.[5] Standing describes the response to precariat society as a politics of inferno characterised by surveillance, invasion of privacy, centrally controlled education policies, hiring and firing, paternalism, distraction, and demonisation.[6] It is not difficult to see similar pressures on Churches as anxiety about survival drives more centralising and standardised strategies which can lead local church leaders and their congregations to feel blamed for numerical decline. Yet precariat is derived from the Latin word, *prex*. This can be translated as prayer, prayer which involves trust and hope in the faithfulness of God. This divine faithfulness is seen in the commitment of the risen Christ to be with and go ahead of his disciples in their Galilee mission.[7] It is trust and hope that reject survivalism and instead display faithful witness, which is engaged, committed and devotional.[8] Much of the recent decline in the size of congregations is not simply the fault of the congregation and clergy. It reflects the educational and social effects of modernity albeit intensified by overzealous religious reform in the past.[9] According to Martyn Percy, 'England has never been an outwardly religious country if Church attendance is anything to go by'.[10] Yet a surprising sense of belonging to the Church remains in secular society seen in local resistance to attempts to close Parish Churches. Furthermore loyalty to the symbols of faith and place remains remarkably strong.[11] Statistics related to engagement with online worship during the early months of the COVID-19 pandemic suggest that nearly a quarter of the population of the United Kingdom accessed such services in sharp contrast to the numbers attending in person worship.[12] Most of this digital engagement was with parish churches with whom worshippers had some existing connection and reflects the reality that 'local churches have a long-term future because for most people everyday life remains local'.[13]

As mentioned in Chapter 2, time in South Africa had

convinced me that theologies are contextual. So ministry in Yorkshire involved becoming sensitive to the context within which I was now rooted, rather than imagining that I could simply transplant a model church from one context to another. Ministry was like learning a new language or cultivating a garden. It involved learning the Yorkshire vernaculars in order to communicate and understand local cultures, stories and settings. It also required time and long-term commitment to these communities as I learned to walk with rather than work for them and thereby began to get to know them rather than simply knowing about them.[14] For example I learned about the damaging history of the church I served when one parishioner told me that as a child she was told to go to the back door of the vicarage because she was from a lower social class. This had left her with a particular view of God and the Church which alienated her. I also came to see that the sudden collapse of traditional industries in South Yorkshire meant that the ex-mining and ex-railway communities in Doncaster felt bereaved and were suspicious of outsiders especially from the south-east of England, whom they blamed for the social pain and cost of the closure of these industries.

MINISTRY AND THE PARISH

Parish ministry in Doncaster therefore meant that I had to learn a new language and set of social skills if my ministry was to be engaged and effective. I had to learn how to read and describe the context before assuming I knew how to be its vicar. This involved researching the local context, its history and character as well as listening to local people inside and beyond the congregation. St Mary's, Wheatley, where I was vicar from 1993–2001, was an inner urban parish of about a square mile comprising about 6,000 residents with a regular Sunday congregation ranging between 65-100 adults with about 20–25 youngsters.[15]

ON YOUR BIKE

Geographically the parish fell into two halves with terraced housing to the north of the main arterial road and the mixed more substantial housing to the south. From its early days in the late-nineteenth century, the suburb had been very desirable but with the demise of domestic service, the rise of suburban living and the high cost of running large properties there was much social change during the post-war period. Many of these properties became bed and breakfast hotels, homes for the elderly and multiple occupancy dwellings, which brought a transient population into the neighbourhood. The challenge that research and conversation raised for the church was how to witness faithfully to the Gospel in this context. As a consequence we decided to focus on worship, nurture and mission. Each needed to reach out to the whole parish and be sensitive to our context. We therefore consulted census records to see the profiles of those living in the parish, mapped any links we had with people in the area and discovered that we had many associate baptised members whose connection with Church we wanted to strengthen. We wanted to be an open and porous community, hospitable to all in the parish so that those unfamiliar with Church could worship with us. To help us do this we held a Prayer and Gift Day in Lent 1993 to raise money for a new public address system and a large projection screen for the front of church. The money arrived, a member of the congregation built the screen and we were able to have book-free projected acts of worship. This was particularly helpful at monthly all age worship during which baptisms took place when we had many visitors in Church.

To enrich nurture we set up Root Groups which met monthly on a Sunday afternoon for Evening Prayer, low key Bible study and a tea party. Root Groups nourished fellowship and provided teams for our mission, whether to deliver leaflets, staff coffee rotas, provide hospitality or arrange celebration events such as Harvest, Epiphany and Easter. Music and singing helped to bind the congregation together and deepen our faith. To help us reach out to the local community we developed visiting teams, welcomed any approaching us for the occasional offices, improved links with local schools, started mid-week and holiday clubs for youngsters, engaged with the local jazz club, patronised local shops, started a Christian Aid Fair and took part in noisy, colourful ecumenical street processions. We found that Christians from overseas working at the local hospital felt welcome at the Church and so we held international evenings where they could share their delicious cuisine with us. We also discovered that visiting and other initiatives developed a sense of responsibility for parish mission among congregational members. As a consequence of these initiatives we decided to renovate the church building in order to make it more flexible. The costs were raised from direct congregational giving and some unexpected legacies. The result was that the congregation grew among local people.

MINISTRY AND LEARNING

Parish ministry can be all consuming and the intellectual work of ministry can be neglected. In particular I had been wrestling for some time with the purpose and place of the Church. Many parishioners spoke of believing, but could not see the point of belonging to the Church. In contrast I felt that the Church was vital to following Jesus Christ but didn't feel that I could make the case for why. I therefore decided to do some further study on the doctrine of the Church in conversation with a contemporary theologian, Stanley Hauerwas.[16] Hauerwas helped me to see that the Church is central and essential to discipleship because it is the community which teaches us the language and practices of faith that form us into Christian witnesses of the Gospel. Learning faith is a form of apprenticeship whereby those who are skilled and experienced in the faith work with Christ to form novices into faithful Christians.[17] This is an education in hearing, hallowing, hosting and hospitality.[18] Through this education we learn to hear the call of God to follow Jesus where we are, we learn to hallow the name of God in our worship and life together, we learn to host the Spirit as we host our communities and we learn to be hospitable to Jesus whom we meet in the stranger.

After eight years in parish ministry I was asked by the Bishop of Doncaster to apply for the post of Director of Ministry in the Diocese of Sheffield, a role which gave me the opportunity to road test Hauerwas's work on church education. One example of such road testing was *Doxa: A Discipleship Course*.[19] The course contributors came from all sections of the Church of England and the course explored the formative and educational character of eucharistic worship rooted in the conviction that participating in worship (*Doxa* in Greek) trains us to become Christian disciples who can live faithfully in God's unfolding story. Another example of this road testing was the establishment of a School of Ministry which met for a Sunday once a month. The purpose of the School of Ministry was to form a learning community of around 70 trainee lay ministers grounded in prayer, fellowship, practice and reflection and becoming theologically competent and confident practitioners able to serve across the Diocese.

MINISTRY AND THE RURAL
In 2014 I became Bishop of Selby and Archbishop's Ambassador for Rural Life and Faith, a challenging role given my own modest experience of rural mission. However

IN MINISTRY

I had some insights about rural life since my mother's family were farmers and I had stayed on the family farm when we were on leave from Uganda. In 1990 *Faith in the Countryside* argued that in rural areas the division between church and community is blurred. This is still the case today and for many rural Christians the 'difficult question is how one can live an openly Christian life in a way that does not alienate those who do not share the faith but attracts (them) through interest into commitment to Christ'.[20] Rural life is increasingly complex and varied. The government designates communities of less than 10,000 people as rural so rural includes town and fringe settlements, villages, hamlets and dispersed dwellings. Rural people comprise 17.6 per cent of England's population with 570,000 living in sparsely populated areas. At present there is a net population increase in rural communities of around 50,000 per annum so rural communities are growing and changing particularly as hybrid modes of working emerge as a consequence of the COVID-19 pandemic. Yet the majority of the rural population are over 45 years old because younger people have to go to the towns and cities for education, jobs and affordable housing. This puts pressure on the viability of small rural schools, churches and other rural services. It also means that established rural populations feel a minority in their communities. This also affects the Church since established rural people have long histories with their Parish Churches but can feel squeezed out or disturbed my enthusiastic incomers who wish to change things. Rural clergy are often caught in the middle of this conflict.

Rural areas also mask poverty and social isolation. In particular social poverty is increasing and afflicts the materially poor and the affluent as age and infirmity isolate more of the rural population and as statutory support services reduce. Loneliness and mental health

ON YOUR BIKE

conditions are the outworking of this isolation. Some years ago the now-defunct Commission for Rural Communities calculated that the rural poor in England numbered the population of Birmingham, yet many visitors to rural areas, particularly in North Yorkshire, would be hard-pressed to recognise this. The rural poor are often invisible and dispersed. For example in 2020-21, 31 per cent of farms had a net farm income of less than zero.[21] For all who live in rural areas, higher transport, property and living costs combined with reduced public services, utilities and employment prospects for the young mean that the pounds don't go as far as in urban areas and younger people have to leave for employment elsewhere. My grandparents lived on a 40 acre mixed farm raising seven children and employing several people. However in recent times the farm couldn't support my bachelor uncle. In 2017-18, 17 per cent of households in rural areas were classified as relatively poor, and 14 per cent as absolutely poor.[22] Yet in rural areas poverty is not simply material. My uncle, now in his eighties is part of a growing elderly population in rural communities of which 22.5 per cent are over 65. He has lived an isolated and solitary life with no private transport. A few years ago my mother phoned him and found that he was suffering from heart problems and needed to go to hospital immediately. Thankfully she was able to contact a local relative and he was taken to the Accident and Emergency Department (A&E). Otherwise things might have turned out differently.

Rural churches in Yorkshire are responding positively to these challenges even though resources are stretched. First, rural churches are embedded in their communities and so rural churchgoers in Yorkshire already know and care for their vulnerable neighbours, which is important now that there are fewer clergy in rural areas. Secondly, rural churches are committed to working together in rural mission. For example, a few years ago the Arthur Rank Centre and Yorkshire Churches Rural Business Support (YCRBS) has partnered to a pilot Rural Isolation Project in Yorkshire. Four churches, two Anglican and two Methodist, were given a modest grant and some training to enable them to start projects which tackled social isolation in their settings. Thirdly, the YCRBS has re-established an ecumenical chaplaincy in the Yorkshire Agricultural Marts where farmers gather. Chaplains provide a listening ear and referral facility for a section of the rural community who can be hard to reach. Fourthly, rural churches support farming charities such as Farming Communities Network (FCN), the Addington Fund and the Royal Agricultural Benevolent Institution (RABI) through giving and fundraising. FCN seeks to befriend isolated farmers, while the Addington Fund helps with housing, and RABI with support grants. Fifthly, rural Church Schools build social capital in dispersed rural villages and towns. Keeping rural schools open is therefore vital for rural communities since if a school closes the community declines as families have to go elsewhere for the education of their children. Sixthly, an increasing number of rural churches with toilet and kitchenette facilities are open during the day for visitors and community activities. Seventhly, through the experience of the COVID-19 lockdown, many rural churches have explored digital worship, nurture and outreach. Looking ahead, a blended approach to on-site and online worship not only has the potential to help churches reduce their costs and carbon footprints, but also provides a window for inquirers along with ministry to the housebound and those who cannot attend in-person Sunday worship for domestic or employment reasons. If the initial research is accurate, virtual engagement with the Church has been higher than normal in-person attendance. A ComRes survey published in May 2020 found that 44 per cent of the population said they prayed regularly and 25 per cent have watched or listened to a religious service during the COVID-19 lockdown of whom one third were aged 18-34.[23]

MINISTRY AND REFLECTION
Ministry and story
More than thirty years' ministry in 'God's own County' has shown me that ministry is forged in worship and story. As Paul Avis comments, the 'Church's apprehension of truth is given, not through steadily more precise and accurate interpretations of its doctrinal formulae, but through its life of worship, prayer, fellowship, service and suffering'.[24] I have learned that Christians are storied people who cannot understand our present without knowing our past. This is why we read ancient Scriptures and follow calendars which recall past people and events.[25] Our Scriptures and history show that we are part of an unfolding story or drama, which binds Christians of all traditions together since we cannot tell our stories without including each other's stories. Parishes with their church buildings are part of this unfolding history. As John Inge and Philip Sheldrake argue, places are more than simply spaces.[26] They are settings of story, identity and belonging. This is particularly true for rural parishes and explains why there is conflict when there is any suggestion of church closure. The church building is a material text telling a community's story and along with rural traditions such as Harvest, Lamas, Rogation and Beating the Bounds signs the sacred in their midst.[27]

Ministry and time
Ministry in Yorkshire in particular has taught me that to make a difference and see change involves long term commitment to people and place. Many parts of Yorkshire have suffered industrial decline and marginalisation

which makes local people suspicious of incomers with bright ideas. It therefore takes time to build trust, gain credibility and learn to share the faith in the vernacular. Such commitment reflects the logic of the Incarnation and Pentecost that God meets people in their own cultures and in their own languages.[28] We learn to discern God in the fabric of life by being where that life is lived, whether this be rural or urban.

Ministry and availability
Yorkshire has also been the most challenging place for me to serve given my limited understanding of local cultures. Yet serving communities and places as a stranger has required a deeper trust in God's call. I am therefore frustrated if I hear ministers mapping out the sort of parish or ministry they are prepared to serve. Ministry is about being available for whatever God requires of us. I have often felt out of my depth in the communities of Yorkshire I have served, yet I have also found that these communities have been my greatest teachers. When we feel vulnerable we discover that God is near and that we are only ever ministry apprentices dependent on local people to help us learn their language and culture.

CONCLUSION
Ministry in Yorkshire, as in Africa, has shown me that love is at the heart of God. God is as Jesus is and Jesus is the self-emptying God who asks everything of us yet also gives us the deepest experiences of grace when we answer that love with our lives. Often I have felt powerless and inadequate as a minister of this Gospel. Yet God, the infinite who works through the finite, has chosen the way of impotence and fragility in order to love and respect the integrity of creation and this gives me hope.

ON YOUR BIKE

Questions for reflection

1. What have you learned about faith and ministry in the places where you have lived and served?
2. Who have been your greatest educators in faith and ministry and why?
3. How have worship and practice shaped your ministry?
4. What sort of commitment and availability is asked of you in your present setting and how are you managing this?

CHAPTER 4

In Suffering

SUFFERING AND SURPRISE

My legs felt like jelly and my heart was in overdrive. Something wasn't right about this ride. I persevered for about a mile thinking that things would settle but they didn't. As I reached the Toll Bridge in Selby I was forced to turn round and slowly make my way back home my heart thumping all the way. I lay down for half an hour and the symptoms eased so I got up and went outside to pick some raspberries. Then as I walked more briskly to the compost heaps at the bottom of the garden my heart started racing again and I felt dizzy. As I sat down I sensed that this was something serious though without any pain it was difficult to know what it was. It had been a stressful few weeks and I had noticed that I was breathing more deeply when climbing stairs and on early morning rides. I assumed that this was a sign of being older and less fit. However this event was concerning so I phoned 111 and arranged to go to the out of hours GP at Selby Memorial Hospital. The doctor took my pulse and looked worried. He told me that I must go at once to A&E in York. So began four months during which I visited A&E nine times with palpitations and had a number of treatments to deal with the situation. Thankfully these interventions together with medicine stabilised my condition. Yet as a fit person used

ON YOUR BIKE

to regular cycling and walking this health hit was a major shock. At times I wondered if I would be able to cycle again. All I knew at this early stage was that this was a life changing experience and that the future would not be as the past had been.

The causes of this condition are not clear. It could be the legacy of one or more viruses I was exposed to as a child in Uganda. It could be the result of the stress of cross-cultural ministry in England over many years. It may simply be the legacy of my ancestors some of whom had heart issues. Thankfully it seems unlikely to be the direct result of cycling since cyclists with conditions like this are extreme sports athletes whereas I am a recreational rider.[1] Nevertheless it has undermined my self-confidence as my body feels more like a stranger rather than a familiar friend. I am having to learn what I am now capable of whereas in the past I could predict fairly accurately how long it would take me to cycle somewhere. In response to Jesus' challenge to love the stranger I am trying to love my strange body and to see this experience as an opportunity to learn more about life and faith rather than regarding it as a curse to be hated.

Yet although the experience has been very testing, I have encountered many angels along the way. Once I had palpitations that took me into York Hospital on the evening before my first early morning consultation at Leeds General Infirmary. In my anxiety I wondered if God had forsaken me since if I were kept in York Hospital I would not get to the Leeds appointment at 9.00 a.m. the next morning and the essential treatment I needed would be further delayed. I was at my lowest ebb, seemingly abandoned and forgotten by God. Yet as I cried out in prayer I recalled the little passageway in the deepest part of Hell mentioned in Canto 34 of the medieval Italian poet, Dante's, *Inferno* in *The Divine Comedy.* Going through this passageway enabled Dante and Virgil to escape from Hell's horrors.[2] As I prayed I also remembered Christ's cry of desolation on the cross using words from Psalm 22, a Psalm which ends with a confession of trust that God will rescue and give the sufferer a future of blessing. My Easter sign turned out to be a Kenyan nurse assigned to my care. As we talked about her country I tried out my poor Kiswahili, one of the languages spoken in Kenya. This developed a bond between us as I told her of my predicament. The upshot was that she persuaded the A&E Registrar to discharge me from hospital at 6.00am that morning. My wife Sue collected me at 6.15 a.m. and we drove to Leeds well in time for the 9.00 a.m. appointment. This Kenyan nurse was one of a number of angels I discovered in the National Health Service many of whom came from Africa.

SUFFERING AND REALITY

Suffering is our response to something which afflicts us and much ministry involves accompanying people in their suffering and helping them to find meaning in this dark journey. At its most basic suffering reminds us that we are in a real world since we do not choose suffering but rather experience it as a response to something beyond us. As such it shows us that we are not in control of our lives and we find this frightening because it subverts the myth of autonomy which is deeply embedded in our culture. Suffering therefore strips us of the self-image we have constructed which, in my case, was of a fit, relaxed and flexible person able to respond to anything life threw at me. Instead for the first time in my life I felt completely helpless with my self-confidence severely shaken. For Christians suffering forces us to decide whether to live from above, that is from God, or be driven by fear and anxiety. Suffering challenges us to graduate from an approach to life which tries to keep control to one in which we slowly discover how to become more trusting, reflective and contemplative.[3]

SUFFERING AND PAIN

Suffering harrows us. As a consequence we want everything to get back to normal with a god who makes everything come out right and rids us of our pain. Yet the stories of Jesus and Israel and the testimony of those who have followed Jesus suggest that this is not the way God works. Pain and struggle are part of the gift of creation. They are forms of discomfort which tell us that we are finite and live with limitations, some of which we can transcend but others of which are necessary to protect us from harm. I recall as a child meeting lepers on an island in south-west Uganda who only knew that their hands were burnt in the fire when they smelt their own burning flesh. Nevertheless pain and struggle can cause suffering and this is where the story of Jesus invites us to trust that God will bring Easter out of our Gethsemanes and Good Fridays. Indeed as his story shows us, it is as we stay with the struggle rather than flee from it that we encounter God in a deeper way. We discover that God is with us in the darkness as well as in the light and that our 'trials are an expression of ardent love not of rejection'.[4] Suffering and love are the two hands of God, the one cradling the head and the other embracing the body. They are God's dual way of relating to us.[5] The one hand allows suffering for the sake of purification and the other brings the joy of union with God. Our suffering is a response to the physical, psychological and spiritual pains of the world as they impact upon us. However it can still become a source of blessing as we learn a deeper trust in God and become more self-aware and more emotionally and spiritually intelligent.

IN SUFFERING

SUFFERING AND FREEDOM

We see this in the story of Job. The book is often read as the classic biblical treatise on suffering yet in fact it does not resolve the problem of suffering. Instead the story claims that God is only known in relationships of trust forged in the struggles of life.[6] This forging often evokes anger in us as we feel our suffering to be unjust and an experience of betrayal since we feel discarded and unvalued. Yet in the very expression of anger we find we are crying out for love and making connection even as we face the dark side of God. Christians, therefore, don't have a solution to an abstract problem of suffering. Rather, Christians belong to a community, the Church, with a story and form of life which promises that God is with us in our suffering and struggles and that these can be the crucible within which love is formed, refined and deepened.[7] As we wrestle with our suffering we discover richer insights on our journey into God even though, like Jacob, we are wounded as we wrestle with the angel of the Lord.[8] Such wrestling is a moment of encounter when we find ourselves in *Beth'el*, the house of God, the place where we meet God.[9] It is the 'Way of the Wound', a re-defining of our understanding of being with the Lord, a journey which is characterised by risk, trust and surrender rather than by a self-preoccupied quest for control. The seventeenth-century friar, St John of the Cross, calls this luminous darkness the dark night of the soul which is not the absence of God but rather God's overwhelming closeness to us in our sufferings and struggles.[10] So before the truth can set us free we need to be liberated from our need to be in control. We have to be lost before we can be found as Jesus taught in the parables of the lost sheep, coin and son in Luke Chapter 15. All this is how God forms us to be with him and with others in ways that love selflessly rather than use people instrumentally.[11]

ON YOUR BIKE

Michael Mayne's unexpected and sudden experience of chronic fatigue syndrome led him to reflect on 'what a sudden, mysterious, knockdown kind of illness does to you and your family ... about a God who stops you dead in your tracks and sets you groping for answers'.[12] For a year he was 'cabined, cribbed, confined, bound in to saucy doubts and fears' and found, like the poet John Donne, that 'as sickness is the greatest misery so the great misery of sickness is solitude'.[13] He learned that illness is always personal and so can't just be fixed technically since the individual must be involved in the healing process. In addition the darkness of suffering showed him how much the close support of others and the rich storehouse of wisdom and strength in the Psalms helped him through the experiences of panic and anxiety. God can be known in the bad as well as good times and as we grow older our privilege is to have 'a true and creative sharing in the nature of a God who himself became powerless and vulnerable', to encounter a waiting, suffering God who is the bearer of redemption even though God's love is diamond hard and costly.[14] His reflections on his suffering help us to see that God knows our suffering inside out and that in suffering we learn more about God than we would if all went well. Consequently we can give thanks for such experiences and see them as occasions when God visits us in a special way. They help us to reflect on what we really want of God and to learn the lessons of our sickness rather than seeking swift healing. Whilst he was ill Mayne discovered, the power of the body to heal itself and the importance of relaxing, reflecting, reviewing and even relinquishing. Like me he had to give up cycling for this period. He also learned the difference between knowing about illness and knowing of illness and how the latter is what enables us to empathise and minister to others.

IN SUFFERING

SUFFERING AND GOD

Former Archbishop of Canterbury, Rowan Williams, argues that God is as we see Him in Christ. The incarnation shows us that God's presence infuses all of creation rather than being an intervening power entering creation from beyond.[15] As such God refuses to be a rival who imposes himself upon us. Instead God weaves his grace throughout creation in ways which enlarge and transfigure creation without destroying it.[16] In Christ, God's choice is always to be for us and so God can be trusted in the darkness as well as in the light, when a cross is carried or when Easter Day happens. Grace wins out not by conquest but by love as God works from the centre of finite life rather than being an outside intruder.[17] To see God in this way means that we are to live as material beings in a material world with all its limitations and pain trusting that God is with us in our suffering.[18]

John V. Taylor argues that God makes creation the agent of its own development. 'God has an end in view which is never abandoned, but no pre-determined route for getting there.'[19] This means that inherent in creation is the risk of pain and suffering which even God cannot escape. In Jesus's story we see the mystery that God who desires to be given away himself suffers.[20] God is afflicted in every experience of suffering as the cost of love. This is why the cross is at the heart of creation since the cross is not simply about God reconciling fallen, sinful humanity to himself but is also about God making atonement with humankind because of the costs on us of God's creation project. In this sense the incarnation, God in the flesh as Jesus, is about God making amends and restoring trust with creation.[21]

Suffering therefore clarifies the meaning of Christmas, since when we suffer we feel helpless like Jesus in the manger. Yet ironically this very powerlessness is powerful since it calls forth care and attention from others in response to our fragility. Suffering also gives us a deeper grasp of the Passion and Easter stories. Like Jesus we wrestle with God as we seek light in darkness and grace in weakness only to be surprised by angels opening the tomb of our suffering to a new quality and depth of life. In this surrender and contemplation we discover how to follow Christ in a new way as we ask 'Who am I for in life?' 'Am I for God or myself?' 'Do I love God for nothing like Job or am I seeking to be in control?' 'Have I built up an ego which needs to be noticed, rather than being willing to follow Christ for nothing?' 'Do I bargain with God in a calculative manner rather than respond with free love?' And in all of this we face the challenge Christ gave to Peter, 'Do you love me more than these?'[22]

Suffering is always personal. It is my suffering. There is no abstract 'problem of suffering'. Each of us suffers in our own way and so the best we can do is to try to empathise with others' suffering by listening to their stories and accompanying them on their quest for meaning. As the late Rabbi Jonathan Sacks comments, 'in the context of a life, a story is not merely fiction. It is the pursuit of meaning', which, in the Judaeo-Christian Western tradition has been framed as the redemption of suffering.[23] For Jews and Christians formed in this tradition 'life is a story. It is our response to the call of suffering in the world'.[24]

SUFFERING AND MEDICINE

In modern life our experience of suffering is profoundly affected by medicine. We therefore experience illness very differently to our ancestors since we believe that medicine should prevent us from suffering. We regard our bodies as machines to be fixed when they go 'wrong' by godlike

IN SUFFERING

doctors and nurses, and the technological achievements of modern medicine make this possible for much of life. So we treat medics as divine technicians or bio-mechanics who we expect to cure us and save us from suffering and we are tempted to believe that anyone with physical, mental or learning difficulties does not have a life worth living. Alternatively we see health professionals as non-directional health bureaucrats who give us information which we don't really understand in order for us to make decisions we don't really grasp in the name of autonomy and choice. In this light suffering seems pointless and should be eliminated rather than mined for enrichment. This is very different from the more ancient view of the doctor and nurse as the person set aside by the community as a sign that we refuse to exclude the sick from our societies and that we care for the sick and suffering by being with them even if we can't cure them.

CONCLUSION

All of us are grateful for the advances in medicine. However suffering is not something which medicine can really address since it is not so much about the body as about how we deal with events in our lives which we dislike and would not choose. Yet such experiences are reality checks and, for late modern societies seduced by the fantasy that we are in control, this is a particular challenge as we have discovered during the COVID Pandemic and as we face with the Climate Crisis. Indeed they cause us to re-evaluate who and what matters most in life according to David Goodhart, since they challenge the privileging of the cognitively able, the head people, by showing us the vital place in a good society of carers and those with practical skills, the heart and hand people.[25] They remind us that we are part of creation with all its limitations and vulnerabilities and show us that the challenge of life is to learn how to live hopefully with finitude and tragedy. As Walter Moberley argues, when discussing the story of Cain and Abel, there is no 'answer' to unjust suffering and the apparent inscrutability of God. However, what matters is our reaction to the reality of this and whether we are able to make the best of life in a world where arbitrary suffering happens.[26] This is what shapes a Christian approach to suffering since we believe that, in Christ, God has entered into suffering and darkness. God can therefore understand our suffering and this gives us hope that our suffering can be creative and redemptive. To stay with our suffering and to stay with others in their suffering, therefore, is not misguided but is about entering more fully into the mystery of the God we see in the passion story of Jesus, the God who refuses to abandon us.

In the LXX version of Genesis 47: 31 we read that 'Jacob worshipped leaning on his staff when he was about to die.' Here was a wounded worshipper who had learned to lean on God in his vulnerability rooting his heart in God rather than being angry about his condition. God had had to erode Jacob's resistance to walking God's way, and through undergoing this trial he learned that God is an under-going God since God goes under our defences to counter the original sin of preferring to hide from rather than wanting God. Like Jacob suffering and struggle are often the way we come to behold God.[27]

Questions for reflection

1. How has suffering shaped, deepened and enriched your understanding of faith and ministry?
2. What is your response to those who doubt God's existence because of suffering?
3. What does the story of Jesus Christ say to you about suffering, discipleship and ministry?
4. How has medicine influenced your view of suffering?

CHAPTER 5
In Company

CYCLISTS TOGETHER

I am a member of Cycling UK which used to be called the Cyclists' Touring Club until the name was changed in 2016. It was founded by Stanley Cotterell on 5 August 1878 in Harrogate with 80 members when the bicycle was opening up new horizons for independent travel. According to its website, the Cyclists' Touring Club set out to identify suitable hotels for its members and include them in members' guides and handbooks. The hotels often had the emblem of a winged wheel to indicate that they would welcome cyclists. In 1936, the Cyclists' Touring Club created a first cycling proficiency scheme in response to increasing cyclists' casualties at the time. This was adopted as a national programme run by the Royal Society for the Prevention of Accidents in 1948. Cycling UK still offers cycling training courses and supports and enables *Bikeability* as well as acting as a cyclists' pressure group to lobby the government on their behalf. It also provides advice, insurance and links to local groups which organise local rides. Cycle UK therefore acts as a sort of umbrella for those who see cycling as vital to the health and wellbeing of our society and yet realise that cycling is a vulnerable mode of transport which needs support and protection.[1]

ON YOUR BIKE

To be a cyclist, therefore, is to be vulnerable. On a road cyclists are vulnerable because they share the highway with larger road vehicles. Cyclists often ride in isolated terrain and so find group rides safer and more rewarding than solo riding which explains the popularity of club and group rides. In addition we cannot learn to ride without the help and guidance of others who have cycled before us. In this sense being a cyclist involves belonging to a community of cyclists, past and present, who help one another to become good and proficient cyclists. In the same way Christians belong to God's company, the Church. Believing is like learning to cycle as we take part in the journey of faith with more experienced believers. Faith is a way of travelling through life with God at the centre, in company with fellow Christians who show us how to belong, believe and behave. Following Christ is also a vulnerable way of life. The constant barrage of cynical comments and stories about congregational decline and religious irrelevance can cause even the most committed Christians to lose their balance. Yet just as cyclists can trump cars in urban traffic with their flexibility and capacity to improvise on a ride, so Christians can surprise sceptics with the quality and character of their witness as they trust in the grace of God.

CHURCH: A CAPACIOUS COMPANY

As a child growing up in Uganda I was inspired by a church characterised by energy, adventure and hope. It was also a community prepared to challenge personal and social abuse, and be sacrificed for the wellbeing of others. The martyrdom of Archbishop Janani Luwum in 1977 and the resistance to Dictator Idi Amin by a young lawyer, John Sentamu, later the first black Archbishop of York, illustrated this very dramatically. In Uganda I saw that Christianity can span all sections of society. Such Christianity was about

IN COMPANY

walking together in the light. Ugandan Christians saw Christianity as an egalitarian faith in which local people and foreigners were equally forgiven sinners and siblings in God's company. This company was international since the Church in Uganda was consciously part of a global and historic church. To be a Christian made one a global sibling in a way that contrasted with nativist politics or abstract ideologies. Christians were relatives not by blood or as comrades in a cause, but because of their shared experience of God's grace. Such companionship was further enriched as local dialects and global languages shared together in the praise of God as an international and intergenerational community which signed that a Gospel was for all.

This vision of the Church as a capacious company of people reflecting the universal love and grace of God was especially important as a challenge to apartheid in South Africa since it countered the apartheid heresy of the Dutch Reformed Church with its attempt to segregate the races in the name of God. The struggle was hard and the Anglican Church in South Africa was itself compromised. However figures such as Archbishop Tutu refused to allow apartheid to triumph and ensured that forgiveness rather than revenge took place following its collapse. Through prayer and commitment to the struggle these Christians showed me cruciform power in action which, though apparently impotent, was actually stronger than its opponents. Such strength in vulnerability transformed my understanding of the church and has enabled me to trust that God's grace is at work even when we feel impotent and vulnerable and that faithful witness rather than success or achievement matters most. Indeed our witness is often clearest when we are at the edge of our resources since it is as our faith is tested that it is strengthened.[2]

ON YOUR BIKE

CHURCH: A SOMEWHERE-EVERYWHERE COMPANY

As mentioned already, to live in time and place means that we are never simply anybody. We are always somebody. For writers such as David Goodhart,[3] Roger Scruton,[4] and Douglas Murray,[5] neglect of this placed identity is at the root of contemporary populist rebellions against cosmopolitan perspectives. For Goodhart socio-cultural politics are more important to most people than socio economic politics; that is meaning and identity matter more than wealth. This is because in his view most people are somewhere people rather than anywhere people with 60 per cent of the British population living within 20 miles of their birthplace. The dominance in public life of secular, liberal, big city baby boomers has given the impression that people have no loyalty to place or idea of what the good life looks like. They assume that modern people simply want a procedural state with basic legal boundaries that enables each unrooted individual to cultivate their own autonomous life. Yet most people have a sociocentric view of life which is limited by time and place. In contrast to those living in London and other metropolitan areas, these somewhere people feel bereaved rather than liberated by fast social and economic change. They feel bypassed by the new meritocratic oligarchy and its promotion of globalisation, its positive spin on migration and its preference for civic rather than ethnic national identity. In particular white working class communities in the North of England feel that they have been neglected and held back. The public services they depend on have been put under stress as a result of the speed and scale of change. Jobs are increasingly part-time, insecure and fluid as the GIG economy of the internet age means that many are no longer 'just about managing' and the working poor have to access food banks. They are a precariat who are unable to move around the country looking for better prospects. For Goodhart 'a rootless, laissez-faire hyper-individualistic, London-like Britain does not correspond to the way most people live ... or want to live.'[6]

For Scruton such sentiments have led to the resurgence of patriotism or *oikophilia,* the love of home and historic identity. He believes that the advocates of globalisation ridicule this love by calling it nationalism. Yet globalisation has led to a loss of trust, attachment and safety in an increasingly stranger society. This disturbs more rooted people who also believe that identity politics is trumping patriotic unity. In Murray's perspective the past few decades have witnessed Europe's cultural suicide. Major demographic change and certain forms of multiculturalism have displaced commonly held norms rooted in the particular socio-political and religious history of Europe. This has led indigenous communities to feel that they have lost their familiar country and so populism reflects their alienation. As the French philosopher, Simone Weil, saw when she imagined a future for France in the face of the anti-humanism of the Nazis, all societies share the need for roots.[7] Without these they will simply be buffeted by the most powerful voices and interests of their era and the poor in particular will be defenceless.

Yet whilst it is true that many in our society feel that their local has been neglected in favour of a more atomistic and abstract vision of identity, British history actually shows us that we are neither anywhere or somewhere people but we are also everywhere people politically and indeed as the Church. Through empire and language we have shaped other cultures across the globe and inward migration from our former colonies is simply the wash back of our own imperial emigration.[8] My own life exhibits this. When I lived in Uganda and South Africa I was both an anywhere and an everywhere person as mentioned earlier.[9] For the past 30 years my public ministry in England has been in Yorkshire and I have become a somewhere person. Yet as part of the somewhere Church of England I remain part of the everywhere global Anglican Communion. As somewhere communities, English Churches embody the historical and contemporary tapestry of the English story. As part of the everywhere Church they also keep the English in relationship with the global and historic Christian community. In this way the Church in England can be a bridge between the somewhere of England and the everywhere of global and historical Christianity.

So while the Church in England must remain faithful to its historic calling to England, woven as it is into the very fabric of English society, it must also challenge shrunken views of English society and our relationship to the wider world and global church.[10] It certainly matters that the English population are made aware that Parliament, the Health Service, the Welfare State, Just War thinking, Education and the Law are all rooted in Christian ethics and reflect our ancestors' attempt to love our neighbour as ourselves in the public institutions of society.[11] Yet as a movement for others, especially one committed to the poorest sections of society, the Church must listen to those who have now found their own voices, such as women, those from the UKME and LGBTI+ communities and those from the Global South. Again this is the logic of Pentecost which shows us that the Gospel can be expressed in all languages and cultures and so is translatable. As discussed earlier, to share the Gospel therefore means that we must first learn the languages of those we meet in order to understand them and engage in conversation. In so doing we affirm the dignity of their cultures and relativise our own.[12] Furthermore, the world is passionately and diversely religious, and to understand this world and avoid major conflict we need to be religiously literate. Such literacy has become less evident in recent times as our culture has lost its religious moorings and secularisation has marginalised religious voices from the public square. Consequently, that space has been colonised by extremist and violent religious voices which attract under-educated, mainly young, men, with chaotic and/or criminal backgrounds by giving them a public stage upon which they can be heroic figures with a moral cause. This leads to a situation in which fundamentalists, atheist and religious, provoke raging religion which is not representative of established religious traditions.[13] Just as the medical, legal or educational communities would not let isolated, rootless and extremist groups or individuals speak for them, so such individuals or groups do not represent the great religious traditions of the world.

CHURCH: A WITNESS COMPANY

So what is the calling of the Christian community today? According to theologian-ethicist, Stanley Hauerwas, the calling of today's Church is to become an embodied apologetic of the Gospel; that is, a visible and practical witness that responds to contemporary questions about the Christian faith and challenges many of the ideals of late modern societies.[14] For example, this witness questions the modern quest for autonomy which actually strips people of their rich and multi-layered identities by reducing them to isolated, rootless individuals who are powerless in the face of the market and the state.[15] In contrast, the Church is a society of siblings whose freedom is expressed in their mutual love and their care for others. The distinctive company of the Church challenges the view that everyone inhabits the same story about reality, instead asserting that we live in a world of

ON YOUR BIKE

competing social stories each claiming to be truthful. The Church makes the claim that its story is truthful because it enables us to live hopefully and realistically in the face of suffering and tragedy, since neither suffering or tragedy are freely chosen, both undermine our autonomy and yet both also prevent us falling prey to self-deception. The story of Jesus, now embodied in the Church, is therefore a truthful story because it is a divine story about peace making and hospitality which suffering and tragedy cannot undermine. This is seen in the Christian tradition of caring for those estranged from society for example by their special needs or long-term ill health conditions as well as caring for neighbours in a distinctively Christian way.[16]

CHURCH: A FRIENDSHIP COMPANY

The Church therefore is best understood as a community of strangers made friends by Christ who themselves are called to befriend strangers in Christ's name. This inclusivity is seen in the sign of baptism which shows the value of all individuals in God's love, whether slave or free, male or female, Jew or Gentile. Such a view of friendship contrasts with the popular view of friendship as 'like meeting like because we like each other, are alike and like the same things'. Instead Christian friendship is seen in practical commitment to others, especially to the vulnerable and the marginal, because God makes strangers into friends. Consequently to follow Christ means being trained to befriend strangers. Our trainers are other mature Christians past and present whose lives show us how to do this. For Anglicans such befriending of strangers is what parish mission is all about.[17] The Greek word *para-oikos* literally means 'those around the house', that is, those who are strangers to the household of the Church. Mission is therefore about God inviting these strangers to become God's friends gathered in the *ekklesia* or Church. In our society this also involves challenging binary notions of sacred and secular since both have their place in Christian believing. We can actually trace the concept of the secular to the fourth-century African theologian, Augustine of Hippo who used this term to describe the era between Pentecost and the Parousia during which the risen Christ by the Holy Spirit is active in the world, but in a hidden rather than explicit way. The Parousia, or Second Coming, as the finale of all things will make public the work of God in Jesus and the Spirit. In the meantime, to live in a secular world is to live by faith rather than by sight, confident that the secular is not the absent but the real, though hidden, presence of God. God is present but is not always presented.

The Church, therefore, is a social sign of the Gospel and lives in the gaze of God's love. God gives creation freedom to be and to become. God gazes upon creation with the love expressed in the crib and cross of Christ and the Church is to be an icon or gesture of this love for creation, a social sign of grace present in a turbulent world. This involves befriending strangers as the test of genuine love. It means listening to others, past and present who are different from us. It means reading and re-reading our Scriptures in order to listen carefully and respectfully to the voices of those embedded within them. It means paying attention to the 'God-thoughts' of ordinary Christians as well as to those of academic theologians since these reflect the tested wisdom of people and congregations forged in the practicalities of faith.[18] In particular it means listening to the voices of those who disagree with us and trying to see why we differ and how we can befriend one another in our disagreements.

ON YOUR BIKE

CHURCH: A CITIZEN COMPANY

Four key events in the recent past have shaken our confidence in the story that our society has been telling itself about progress and the world becoming more like us. The first was the terror attacks of 11 September 2001 when the Twin Towers in New York were destroyed and many of us were woken up to the rise of Islamism and the rejection of west is best. This also gave those hostile to religion the excuse to equate religion with violence. The second was the financial crash of 2008 which saw the collapse of turbo, or casino, capitalism and the rejection of a banks-know-best credulity. The third was Brexit in 2016 which saw the rise of popularist politics and, as we noted above, the challenge to anywheres (the minority metropolitan liberal elites) by the somewheres (the provincial, conservative majority). It represented a rejection of bosses know best. Finally in 2019 the COVID-19 pandemic spread rapidly across the world revealing globalisation's shadow side, yet at the same time showing the primary importance and fundamental value of community and the common good.[19] Taken together these events have shaken western assumptions about the good life and the belief that the world is getting better, that people are getting better, that life is improving and that in time all people will become like those of us who live in the so called developed countries. In short they have exposed the vulnerability of liberal ideas of progress, of agreed and shared human rights and a pragmatic approach to life.

According to Rowan Williams, this liberal dream, though rooted in the Judeo-Christian inheritance, has now hollowed out the latter and thereby stripped people of a meaningful life, comprised of rich communal identities. All we are left with are shopping, consumerism and a stranger society of autonomous competitors in a battle of all against all in the market state.[20] The climate emergency challenges this dream still further as careless consumption is damaging creation itself. Instead of being tenants in God's world we see ourselves as its owners without any limits to our quest for affluence. We have thereby lost a sense of the inter-connectedness of all things and the biblical language of covenant and care has been replaced by the market language of contract and consumption with no compelling vision of the common good.[21] In contrast the Church, though broken and humiliated, points to a truly liberal society as a sign or gesture of the good life which God seeks for all people. The Church, properly, is a foretaste of what it means to live within the commonwealth of God. This is why the first responsibility of the Church is to be itself as the social life of Jesus today.[22]

The Church can only gesture at what the good society looks like yet it still remains a sign of hope since it is rooted in God's life. It thereby offers a vision of what characterises a divinely infused community and civic life. This is why the New Testament Church used the Greek word *ekklesia* meaning a Citizens' Assembly to describe itself. In so doing it radically re-imagined the *ekklesia* of the Greco-Roman world and the Jewish synagogue. Both were exclusive assemblies of free males. In contrast the Christian *ekklesia* was a community of males and females, girls and boys, slaves and free, rich and poor, Jews and Gentiles. In short it was a sign of the divine good life which we call the Reign of God, the fullness of life. Here was a gesture, a worked example of how to live well in community and civic life, a powerful evangelistic sign in the very diversity of people it attracted.

This distinctive citizenship became less clear when the Roman Emperor, Constantine, converted to Christianity and the relationship between church and civic life became more complex. Christianity was now no longer one sect among many in the Roman Empire but was the imperial faith. Consequently, to be a citizen of heaven and of this newly Christian Roman Empire was less clear cut once as these two citizenships were conflated. This led the third-century North African thinker, Tertullian, to question what Athens has got to do with Jerusalem? Yet one thinker who did not share Tertullian's scepticism was the fourth-century thinker Augustine of Hippo.[23] His book *The City of God* is an attempt to show Christians how to live as citizens of heaven in the earthly city. Augustine is a theologian of time and contingency. In both *The Confessions* and in *The City of God* he seeks to help Christians live in a finite, fallible and fallen world (the earthly city) as resident aliens rather withdrawing from that world in order to embody the perfect Church (the heavenly city). In so doing he rejected the views of two religious groups of the time, the Donatists and the Manicheans. The Donatists believed it was possible to live perfectly in this corrupt world as segregated holy sects. The Manicheans believed that the world was bad and therefore engagement with it was to be avoided. Both were about social withdrawal and a refusal to take responsibility for shaping the good life of their societies. Augustine argued against them that a Church in time is a Church seeking to live faithfully in this finite and fallen world. It should not withdraw from public life and thereby weaken it as their Roman pagan critics assumed they would. These pagans believed that Constantine's conversion had undermined the character of the Roman Empire and its religious traditions leading to its collapse. In contrast, Augustine argued that it was the pagans rather than the Christians who caused this collapse since their commitment to public life and office was motivated by the quest for personal glory and a noble legacy rather than the pursuit of the common good. The Roman Empire consequently collapsed because it had no public service but was rather ruled by a self-serving elitist group. Christians, in contrast, showed true public service, which is the service of and for all, especially the poor and weak. In doing so they displayed a sign of how God wishes all to live in community and civic life.

CONCLUSION

Christians are an everywhere-somewhere community rather than an anywhere community, a global and local company following the way of Jesus within all cultures and sensitive to local history. Place, history and culture matter to the Christian faith given its incarnational character, yet the incarnation, God with us in Jesus Christ, also embraces all cultures as settings for God's salvation as Pentecost demonstrates. Christians are also an improvising company since there is no ideal Christian blueprint for either church or society which can escape the contingencies of history, community and context. Yet they are also an embodied apologetic and for Anglicans this is what the parish system represents. As parochial communities Christians are kept alert to the fact that Jesus is predominantly encountered in the mundane and normal rather than in the spectacular and special. Finally, they are a company of citizens of both heaven and earth who trust that God is a loving, self-giving reality. This reality sustains all that exists yet 'does not guarantee for himself a place in the created world, a place alongside other agents ... [and]so is visible only when a human life gives place, offers hospitality to God, so that this place, this identity becomes a testimony'.[24] This God, in Christ, is present in fleshly existence since 'God has made us to live as material beings in a material world and has made us, therefore, as creatures who have to learn to live in that kind of world.'[25]

ON YOUR BIKE

Questions for reflection

1. What is most important to you about the Church and why?
2. In what ways are you a somewhere and in what ways are you an everywhere Christian?
3. How is your local church an embodied apologetic for the Gospel?
4. As a minister how are you forming Christians to be citizens of heaven who live in the earthly city?

CHAPTER 6
In the Lead

VISIONARY CYCLING

It is relatively easy to become a proficient cyclist. Most people find riding a bicycle quite simple and for those who find balancing is difficult or who want a different cycling experience there are tricycles and recumbents. I learned to ride a bicycle by watching more experienced riders and letting them show me how to gain the skills of a confident and competent cyclist. These were my leaders who showed me the wonder of cycling, and one of them was my younger brother, though he also showed me that leaders take risks and can make mistakes. On one occasion, after doing their A levels, he and two friends decided to take their bikes by train to Rome and then cycle back to England camping along the way. They set out with all the necessary luggage for touring packed into paniers and strapped onto the top of their cycle racks and peddled into London to get the train to Europe. Thereafter we heard very little from them until they arrived in Nice when we had an urgent phone call from my brother describing a near fatal encounter with the sluice gates of the city. Apparently they had arrived at Nice and were enjoying the beach when the weather turned stormy. Looking for a place to shelter they saw some wooden gates with the phrase '*Defense de Stationer!*' written on them but because their French was poor they parked themselves there without concern. The storm broke with heavy rain and they felt safe until suddenly they heard creaking from the opening gates and all the water from the

ON YOUR BIKE

drains of Nice poured out taking two of the bikes out to sea. Only my brother managed to hang onto his bike. As a result the rest of their time in Nice was spent in a modest hotel with upset stomachs from imbibed dirty water before they were feeling well enough to get a train back to England minus two bikes. Listening to the stories of their exploits I felt inspired to cycle. but I was also given an object lesson in its risks and potential failures. I learned that leaders don't always get things right so true leadership includes appropriate humility and openness to learning. As the late Jonathan Sacks said, 'failure is the supreme learning experience and the best people, the heroes, are those most willing to fail.'[1] The result was that I bought a bike to commute to Harefield Hospital when I worked there as a Care Assistant after university and later became a cycling ordinand, curate, vicar and a Diocesan Director of Ministry. I now have a tabard with my episcopal coat of arms, the three swans of Selby, inscribed with 'Biking Bishop of Selby'.

As in any sport, it is easy to believe that the real leaders are those at the top of their game, those with the biggest public profile and media accolades. However in many cases we are inspired to cycle by those known only to us. They are ordinary cyclists whose infectious passion attracts us and whose patient encouragement gives us confidence to get on our bikes. This is leadership distributed at ground level rather than centralised direction by an elite of well-known experts. These local leaders are passionate about cycling; its freedom, health benefits and sociality that they share with cycling novices. In this sense cycling has affinities with the Church. In the Church, leadership is most embodied in local settings and among ordinary people. These leaders show us the way of faith and inspire us to join them on this journey. In my own experience as a vicar and now a bishop, I have become convinced that working with local leadership is essential if change is to happen at ground level.

IN THE LEAD

LEADERS AND RUDDERS

Central to Christian leadership is the idea of steering a boat. The Greek word *kubernesis*, translated as leadership or administration in 1 Corinthians 12:28, is about having one's hand on the rudder. As someone who has been called by God in the Church to be a deacon, priest, bishop, tutor, curate, vicar and trainer, I have been involved in leadership for much of my adult life. Sometimes my leadership task has been to help an individual or a community see a new future and to find ways of realising it. Often it has involved walking with people on their life journeys and helping them to clarify what their calling is and how that can be fulfilled and enriched. On the way I have learned much from inspirational leaders many of whom have been on the edges of the Church whether in deeply rural villages in South Africa or in the parishes of South and North Yorkshire. They have been my greatest educators as they have challenged me to follow Christ whatever the outcome, sharpened my sense of calling and shown me that it is at the margins and in our fragility that we discover God most profoundly. I think of Faisi, whose name in English means Faith, who worked for my parents in Uganda and looked after me as a child. Though she had little formal education she was able to read Luganda her mother tongue. Often she would invite me to sit with her on the stoop of our house as she prayed and read her large, black Luganda Bible. There was a simple and inspiring integrity about her devotion which meant that when my mother challenged me to read my Bible and pray at boarding school in Edinburgh, Scotland, this seemed an obvious thing to do. More recently inspiration came from Andy and Olive Coupe who lived in a pre-fabricated rented house in Wheatley Park, Doncaster for most of their married life. They were from the West Country and had come to faith as younger people. Both worked at the local railway works in Doncaster called The Plant, though when I knew them they were long retired. Tragically all their offspring died in childbirth yet they never seemed bitter but instead looked for ways to help others. In Andy's case this involved using his technical skills in church. Towards the end of their lives both had health issues and Andy lost a leg to gangrene. Ever the extrovert, he relished taking his false leg off in front of visitors, especially children, and showing how it fitted his stump whilst giving his ever fresh testimony about walking with Christ each day with joy and hope. Olive simply used to smile! Faisi, Andy and Olive helped me to see that self-giving service is at the heart of Christian leadership, service which ensures that we steer others towards the deeper love of God.

LEADERS AND MEMORY

Some years ago I was listening to someone on the radio talking about President Kennedy's visit to NASA during the great space race of the time. Kennedy came upon one of the cleaners and asked him what he was doing: He answered, 'I'm helping to put a man on the moon!' That man knew his calling and task and it is this clarity of calling and task which should characterise Christian leadership. Such leaders also help the Church remember through story and sign that we live in a world alive with God's saving grace. They remind the Church that Christians are in a prophetic play which bears witness to the saving action of God in the world. The role of the prophet in Israel was to challenge Israel to perform their prophetic part properly. Indeed as Kierkegaard said 'when a king dies, his power ends. When a prophet dies, his influence begins'. The prophet held the community accountable to the script of that drama to ensure that their performance was faithful rather than fickle, a performance which truly exhibited the agenda of the Lord. For example in Isaiah Chapter 61 the prophet proclaims his summary of God's reign which he believes to be the Lord's agenda for Israel. This is an agenda of healing, liberty, judgement, justice, joy and praise and echoes the theme of Isaiah Chapter 49 which was usually attributed to the earlier sixth-century prophet known as Second Isaiah. It's as if the later prophet was saying to the community: 'Look up. Once again I'm reminding you of the same compelling vision as my earlier predecessor who was calling to mind the great themes of our core story which reach back to Moses and the ancestors. Your call is their call, a call to live this vision as a witness to the Lord whose people you are.'

Church leaders are therefore agents of memory whose task is to challenge God's people to see themselves in an ongoing prophetic drama which speaks about God and God's vision for the world. This reminds me of the role of Archbishop Tutu during the apartheid days in South Africa. Tutu challenged the churches to perform their part in this play by living in ways that spoke God's story to South Africa's apartheid society, a story in which black and white are of equal worth and dignity and should have equal rights. Such a challenge was costly and continues to be since it involves a change of heart and life but it is the way others come to see what it means to live in a world alive with God's saving grace. This is the pastor leading as prophet reminding the people of God of their prophetic calling to represent a word from the Lord to their society. *Anamnesis,* the Greek word translated as remember in the Gospels and in Paul's account of the Lord's Supper, means much more than simply recollection. It speaks about entering into the drama as actors who so live their parts that they become the part they play. This is worship in which we offer all of our lives, struggles, joys and afflictions, to the Lord. As James Chapter 5 suggests, prayer, praise and penitence shape the way the Church remembers before whom we live and shows us how to take part in God's transforming drama since we pray, praise and confess in Jesus' name. Such worship is not simply pointing to Christ but is participating in his meaning for the world. As we do so we discover life in the fountain of God's love.

LEADERS AND PUBLIC MINISTRY

Christian leaders enable the water of God's love to infuse and shape the Church so that it can be transformed into a foretaste of God's Kingdom on earth. Leaders pray, praise and confess to help the Church pray, praise and confess better. And as those ordained to represent this leadership in public, they have particular responsibilities to sign this Gospel love. I think this is why James uses the Greek word *sozo*, the salvation word, to speak of healing in Chapter 5 of his letter as the elders anoint the sick. Anointing, like baptism and Eucharist, is a gospel sign which the elders or leaders of the Church do on behalf of the Church. As the sick, whether individuals or communities, are placed by prayer in the fountain of God's saving love they experience the healing of God. So ministry means being willing to serve sick, marginalized communities as a sign that they are at the centre of the healing or saving fountain of God's love.

LEADERS AND PASTORAL MINISTRY

Christian leaders are to help the Church embody Christ's way, the way of humility in which 'the Son of Man came not to be served but to serve and give his life as a ransom for many'.[2] This way may actually be more challenging for extroverts than for introverts since extroverts though appearing bold, charismatic, energetic, active, assertive and adventurous are not necessarily the best leaders since they may be using other people to meet their own needs. In contrast introverts need people less so, whilst they can appear to be shy, quiet, reserved and cautious, they may better empower others and get results by working with others in more selfless ways.[3] Such humble pastoral leadership is self-aware, attentive and open to change. It invests in relationships which build trust, foster collaboration and serve the whole organization rather than particular interest groups within it. It is leadership as an art rather than a technique and makes sense of why the term pastor is the main leadership word in the New Testament. Indeed according to the ancient Chinese philosopher, Lao Tzu, 'a leader is best when people hardly know that he exists, not so good when people obey and acclaim him, much worse when they despise him. Fail to honour people and they fail to honour you. Of a good leader who talks little when his work is done and his aims fulfilled, they will say "we did it ourselves".'[4]

LEADERS AND CHANGE

Christian leaders are to guide the Church through change. This is what Mark Carney calls Values Based Leadership. It is participative leadership committed to transformation which passionately engages people with a shared purpose, enthusing and explaining so that they grasp the way ahead. In particular such leadership is characterized by emotional intelligence.[5] We see something of this in Luke Chapter 4 where Jesus engages his listeners by quoting Isaiah Chapter 61 in order to root his change message in Israel's prophetic tradition and to explain through the story of the widow of Zarephath and Elijah that this prophetic way is for all people, aware as he is that in making this connection he is touching a raw nerve in his hearers. His message is that what the prophets hoped for is present in Christ who shows us that we now live in a new world and a new era. This is the time of the Messiah's Manifesto, a mandate or commandment, which shows us practically what it means to live and witness in a world alive to God's grace. It is a

ON YOUR BIKE

Manifesto of the sort of change Jesus is bringing about and represents the excellence of love which Paul speaks about in 1 Corinthians 13. Christian leaders in particular are called to exemplify this excellence as the Church's public representatives. Consequently 'no-one does more harm in the Church than the one who having the title or rank of holiness acts evilly'.[6]

Change is always disturbing and disruptive and in today's world the speed of change is particularly disorientating intensified by the crisis of trust evoked by social media, popularist politics and intense horizontal comparisons as a sense of accountability to God dissipates.[7] This is why many people struggle with change. Good leaders help their communities to see that change is part of life and enable them to be agents of that change. They value the input of others.[8] They must also be realistic about the speed of change in the light of the people, places and situations they serve. When St Mary's, Doncaster, began to explore a building project we asked a local and well-established Church member who was an artist to paint an impression of the renovated Church building. Although it took time his painting won over the congregation and gave confidence to those anxious about the enthusiasm of a spendthrift young vicar. They could now visualise the change and see how it would improve the mission of the Church to the parish. In a similar way the Parochial Council took a year to pray and explore whether children should receive holy communion before confirmation. This process enabled all voices to be heard and for the decision to be unanimous

LEADERS AND CHARACTER

In my experience good leadership is primarily about calling and character and secondly about competence and chemistry.[9] Calling is from God through the Church rather than personal ambition. Character is the mark of a person and reveals the sort of person they are in their manner of life. This is why the most exemplary Christian leaders have not necessarily been the most competent nor the easiest to get on with. I think of Charles de Foucault who turned his back on his military calling to become a Trappist monk eventually going to live as a hermit in Algeria. His vision was to establish a community there but no one joined him. He didn't preach to the local Berbers but instead lived as an example of faith, a sermon so powerful that it led to his assassination in 1916. I think of Nancy Charton, the first woman to be ordained priest in 1992 in South Africa. Nancy was willing to accept the disciplines of her Church until it could accept her calling to be a priest. She did this with humour, commitment and courage. Her ministry through St Bartholomew's, in Grahamstown, included outreach to local prisons, work with GADRA, support of young parents, protest against apartheid through Black Sash and faithful pastoring of her congregation. Nancy died a few years ago aged 90 plus, having continued to minister in her retirement well into her eighties. Both Charles de Foucault and Nancy Charton show that character and calling are primary since they build trust and root an understanding of power in the self-effacing power of Jesus. Competence and chemistry, though important, are secondary in Christian leadership.

LEADING AND TEAMS

Leadership is also about team building. This is often challenging since the choice of team members in local churches may be limited rather than a dream-ticket Belbin team. Growing good teams can also be hard for those who like to lead from the front. Richard Hytner calls these leaders 'A' leaders who may be tempted to lead unilaterally and use their power to shut down dissent, thereby undermining team morale and coherence.[10] In contrast those leading from the second chair, the *Consiglieri,* have a more subtle and open leadership style involving emotional intelligence, coaching gifts, counselling insights and educating skills. These skills build good teams and ensure that 'A' leaders make better, more considered decisions. In a world disrupted by the impact of new technology such subtle leadership skills may be more suitable for the emerging digital world in which traditional hierarchies are being disrupted.[11]

Consequently leaders who welcome conversation, conflict and dissent build productive teams that can explore and test issues in order to reach real consensus. This is often very a difficult business since leaders and their teams are regularly faced with wicked and hard problems rather than simple ones. Wicked problems are never solved to the satisfaction of everyone. For example it is nearly impossible to get agreement about sexuality. In this case leadership aims to achieve the widest consensus while accepting the inevitability of dissent. Hard problems, in contrast, can be resolved with time, research, patience and tenacity, for example working out how to reduce the carbon footprint of a church. The process is challenging but patient and informed debate can bring consensus. Simple problems, such as what time is best to open the church before a service, are relatively easy to resolve with good will and practical judgement.[12] However, in my experience, there are few simple problems in ministry which is why wisdom is so important for all leaders.

LEADERS AND WISDOM
Good leadership requires wisdom rather than simple technique. The ancient Greeks used the word '*phronesis*' to convey this practical wisdom. Practical wisdom is the wisdom needed to lead a community in an ever changing world. For Anglicans this practical wisdom is rooted in reflection on the Church's Scriptures, tradition and reasoning. It is a form of spiritual direction in which 'theologically centred

leadership' shapes the cure of souls. Former Archbishop of Canterbury, Rowan Williams, exemplified such wise leadership. He was often criticised for not leading more assertively and definitively, yet his pastoral letters to the Anglican Communion, rooted in Scripture, tradition and sound learning, and his vision of Christian leadership as synodical rather than singular, demonstrated his practical wisdom. Wise leadership persuades rather than coerces, combining personal holiness with a rich grasp of Christian wisdom. As mentioned above wise leaders resist simplistic solutions to complex issues instead listening and learning from others, even those they disagree with. Jim Collins calls these leaders 'level five leaders' who are characterized by personal humility, professional excellence and organizational or institutional commitment.[13]

LEADERS AND STORY

Christian leadership is a narrative art. It involves helping communities to recognize and explore their stories as part of the great Story of God's creating and saving activity. A good example of such a storyteller is Deborah in Judges Chapter 5. Here she sings the story of her people in a way that enables them to see how their present emerges from and is resourced by what they have learned of God's story present in the history of his people. She reminds me of childhood memories of the Nakayima Shrine on the top of Mubende Hill, just over two miles outside the town of Mubende in Uganda. The Shrine is marked by a Nakayima tree with large root buttresses which form nooks and fissures at the base of the tree. This hill was where the wise woman of Mubende, Nakayima, held court. Her role was to dispense wisdom so that her community could see their present predicaments within the greater story of their tribe and its gods. Deborah and the wise woman of Mubende show us that narrative leaders walk with their communities rather than act for them. They tell stories that help their communities focus upon the assets God has given them rather than on their deficiencies.[14] For example ministry in rural communities can appear much more fragile than much suburban ministry. This often leads to a sense of diminishment amongst rural church leaders. However good leaders can see that rural churches are often much more porous than urban churches with church members so engaged in both community and church life that it is not easy to see where church and community begin and end. This is a story of community investment by rural churches which may not equate to regular attendance, but has greater proportionate impact on such communities.

LEADERS AND OVERSIGHT

Malcolm Grundy argues that Christian communities need oversight leaders who face outward and inward. Their outward facing role is to build coherence in a fragmented world and enhance the common good by developing trust across the wide range of their public relationships and partnerships. Their inward facing role is to ensure that change has the consent of the people of God and is grounded in Scripture, tradition and sound learning. This is a very challenging task since oversight leaders are often deceived about what is going on given the amount of information they receive and the difficulty of getting feedback from those they watch over because of the power relationship between them.[15] However if such leaders listen and learn from those they supervise they can foster a trust and openness which frees people to tell them the truth as they see it and this sets up good conditions for wise leadership.

CONCLUSION

Leadership can be heroic, entrepreneurial, managerial, charismatic, strategic, narrative, relational, servant, shared, reflective and institutional.[16] Different church settings will need different leadership styles, which are not simply focused on formal leadership roles, but are distributed throughout the Church. Nevertheless the example of Christ shows us that strong, faithful and humble pastoral leadership committed to Christlike transformation must be at the heart of Christian ministry.[17] Such leaders embody holy pastoral service rather than authoritarianism and build trust.[18] They represent theologically-centred leadership which is committed to prayer and to the study of the Bible and Christian tradition so that they can offer apt and fruitful teaching to congregations.[19] Like Jesus, they embody 'dirty footed leadership' which finds God in the lowliest of settings yet sees there a world 'charged with the grandeur of God'.[20]

Questions for reflection

1. Which Christian leaders have inspired you most and why?
2. How has your leadership, formal or informal, helped to steer your church in the ways of Christ?
3. What style of leadership do you prefer and what styles of leadership do you find yourself exercising?
4. How is shared, storytelling leadership evident in your church?

CHAPTER 7
In the Spirit

CONTEMPLATING CYCLING

Cycling encourages contemplation, that stilling of the surface, self-conscious mind to allow the deep mind's wisdom to surface and illuminate.[1] Whether riding solo or with others, the cadence of pedalling and the rhythm of a ride allow the mind to ruminate and reflect in ways that nourish the spirit. I have often started a ride with a sermon or address to prepare and a sense of frustration and inadequacy about what I can offer. Yet as I ride ideas start to flow, structure emerges and by the time I return home the talk is prepared and simply needs to be put into a script. I have also taken biking retreats, or prayer cycles, and found them to be fruitful times of contemplation providing hours of uninterrupted freedom and quiet to pray and deepen one's devotional journey. Cycling is a very physical activity during which we experience the silence and sounds of nature along with the noise of the urban soundscape and see spectacular rural and cityscapes as well as encountering signs of human creativity and carelessness. In the New Testament spirituality means walking in the Spirit, a social and material experience as the Church, the tangible Body of Christ. It is a journey with others, past and present, to the Father through the Son in the Spirit and since we believe in an incarnational

IN THE SPIRIT

faith a key way in which we live in the Spirit is through our senses. Like cycling Christian spirituality as life in the Spirit involves contemplating embodied life in conversation with the Spirit. It is about discovering the presence of God in the silence, sound, sights and signs of the material world and therefore, like cycling, is a sensory experience. In this chapter I want to explore life in the Spirit in this way aware that there are readers who will feel excluded from some of these reflections due to limitations of sight and hearing. I therefore offer these thoughts in a spirit of conversation inviting these readers to share how their experience can enrich and challenge my own.

LIFE IN THE SPIRIT AND SILENCE

With my father's untimely death in 2000 from pancreatitis I met silence. First I met the silence of his corpse which spoke of an absence. Second there was the silence of the gathered family in the face of the mystery of death. Thirdly there was the silence of God from whom no simple answers emerged, though the moment of his death at sunrise on a Sunday morning spoke about Easter hope. Silence is when we have come to the end of ourselves.[2] It reflects our contingency and finitude when we reach the limit of our capacities and have no more to say. Silence therefore gestures to something beyond ourselves and beyond our grasp of reality. It points to mystery and gestures to the presence of God in life. According to Maggie Ross, the practice of silence also enables us to learn to be more attentive and contemplative, to wait, abide and listen in ways which strip us of our self-preoccupation and need to have 'experiences' and instead lets God meet us as an unexpected gift in fresh and deep ways which go beyond the rational mind.[3] Indeed this may be why all the major religious traditions teach that we are nearer to the divine in our unconscious than when we are awake. The dream-inspired compassionate courage of Joseph, husband to Mary, not to follow his culture's convention and divorce her when he discovered she was pregnant by someone else, exemplifies this.[4]

Yet silence in itself is not always a virtue. As I saw in South Africa during the apartheid era, silence can be imposed by the powerful upon the vulnerable in ways which hide abuse and this is why many minorities today are suspicious about silence. So sometimes silence needs to be challenged rather than celebrated. Yet on other occasions silence is the only appropriate response when we recall events such as the Shoah or Holocaust or the industrial massacres of twentieth-century World Wars.

BIBLE AND SILENCE

According to Diarmaid MacCulloch, a good deal of the biblical tradition is ambivalent about silence.[5] He points out that in the Old Testament silence is a sign of defeat and death: 'What profit is there in my death if I go down to the Pit? Will the dust praise you or tell of your faithfulness?'[6] It is seen as a sign of impotence exemplified in the silence of the idols when confronted by Elijah on Mount Carmel: '"O Ba'al answer us!" But there was no voice and no-one answered.' It is a sign of judgement: 'My God, my God why have you forsaken me ... O my God I cry by day but you do not answer.' It is a sign of suffering and struggle witnessed to in the tradition of the Suffering Servant in Isaiah: 'He was oppressed, and he was afflicted yet he opened not his mouth: like a lamb that is led to the slaughter and like a sheep that before its shearers is dumb, so he opened not his mouth.'

Silence in the Bible is also a sign of mystery and awe as the four dots '....' of the Tetragrammaton show and which are represented in the Hebrew Bible by the letters YHWH.[7] This silence was the response to Moses' request for the

IN THE SPIRIT

Lord's name. It is a silence before the unsayable which resists the human desire to name and thereby control God. Silence can also be ambiguous. In the Gospels Jesus is both the end and also the embodiment of God's silence as he is the Messiah no longer secret. Yet the character of his Messiahship involves the silence of the Suffering Servant at his trial, the apparent silence of God in the face of his unjust death and burial and, for Mark, in the resurrection silence.[8] Christ is the undefended person who stands silent before God and humanity trusting God in his vulnerability. In Matthew Chapter 6, Jesus also advocates silent prayer in contrast to Pharisaic practice whose roots were in the public prayer protests of the second century BC Maccabean Revolt. He himself withdrew to pray in the quiet and clarified his calling in the silence of the temptation battles of the desert.[9] As Jesus stands before the otherness of God and in obedience to the strangeness of God he learns how to love that God for nothing.

DESERT AND SILENCE

The example and teaching of Jesus, according to MacCulloch, show us why the Church has valued silence in the practice of prayer as a way of loving God and neighbour. For example following Constantine's conversion in the fourth century and the decline of persecution many now regarded the solitary, silent battle against the devil as the highest calling of the Christian. Called white martyrs, these monks and nuns were the top spiritual athletes of their day who discovered a serenity which they called *apatheia* as they faced the silence of God in the desert. As they sought 'to be perfect or complete as your heavenly father is perfect or complete' they discovered in the silence and struggle how to love God and others for nothing.[10] And this ongoing practice of silence and struggle can be seen in Carthusians with their walled gardens and individual cells, in Carmelites such as Teresa of Avila and John of the Cross exploring the Dark Night of the Soul, in Trappists who speak only when absolutely necessary and in Jesuits whose Ignatian Exercises are undertaken in silence. It also continues among Protestants in the evangelical quiet time and the silent meetings of the Quakers and in the Orthodox tradition of writing icons using the practice of Hesychasm or silence/stillness to breathe the Jesus Prayer as they write.[11] Silence, therefore, is not an escape from life but a challenge to grow in love by renouncing our attempts to compete with God and one another.[12] As Jesus found in the desert, silence is not about fleeing from God but about being drawn more fully into our calling as children of a loving God in order to love with purity of heart. This is why Isaac of Nineveh says that we must 'love silence above all things because it brings you nearer to the fruit that the tongue cannot express.'[13]

LIFE IN THE SPIRIT AND SOUND

Some years ago as I was cycling around Northumberland near Alnmouth I remember thinking that this was probably the nearest I would get to the soundscape most people experienced until the nineteenth century. There were animal noises, wind rustled the trees, the sound of running water and occasionally the toll of a bell. Before the Industrial Revolution life was relatively quiet for most of the time. This contrasts sharply with the experience of today's urban dwellers who live in a very noisy world mainly caused by human behaviour. Our public soundscape is pumped full of mall music, traffic, adverts and people talking or shouting, while personal soundscapes are often full of TV or mobile phone sound.[14]

BIBLE AND SOUND

Israel and Christianity must take some responsibility for this. Indeed Diarmaid MacCulloch regards Israel's history as a celebration of noise. For Israel, noise was a sign of life whereas silence spoke of death. Noise was a sign of divine power rather than impotent idolatry. Sound meant Yahweh was communicating whether by commanding creation into being in Genesis Chapter 1 or as the noise of heaven in 1 Kings Chapter 22, as a cosmic theophany in Psalm 18, as the praise of creation in Psalm 19 or as the still small voice speaking to Elijah in 1 Kings 19: 12. Temple worship with its festivals, orality ('Hear O Israel...'), its sacrifices and money changing was noisy. Indeed the meaning of Israel's name as 'the one who argues or struggles with God' can be seen in the Psalms and in stories such as Job. According to Daniel Hardy and David Ford 'praise perfects perfection by glorifying God'.[15] In the noise is doxology and early Christians were sound people since Jesus is God's speech in the flesh. For Christians, in the beginning is sound, Word, rather than text or anything else and Jesus displays God's communicative agenda as a public Messiah, teacher and disputant.[16] The Church also has a vocal role. In Matthew the Church is called to make disciples which includes teaching the faith. In Acts, early Christians refuse to be silent about Jesus as Messiah when arrested, for example after the very noisy experience of Pentecost, whilst the Book of Acts itself is a collection of public addresses or sermons about Jesus preached by the apostles. For John of Patmos, God's voice is like the sound of many waters accompanied by the playing of harps and the heavenly choir singing the praise of God.

The Bible is therefore a 'soundscape of poems, prophecies, stories and exhortations laughed over and cried over down the centuries ... brought to life when it is

ON YOUR BIKE

read aloud, proclaimed and signed, talked about.'[17] In it we hear the sound of lament in the story of Abel's murder and in the weeping of Rachel over her children,[18] in the pathos of Jephthah's virgin daughter facing death at her father's hand and in the Book of Lamentations grappling with Jerusalem's destruction.[19] We hear Jesus weeping over Jerusalem and crying out on the cross to voice his sense of abandonment by God. We hear Easter in the sounds of the Resurrection, earthquakes and angelic voices. Yet for Christians, this biblical soundscape represents the Church's witness to God's hopeful future as it sings its song of freedom with the music of the angels.[20] Easter means that we can join in the liturgy of heaven which sin had stopped us from hearing.[21] This is why Patrick Kavanagh calls the Resurrection a 'laugh freed for ever and ever' .It is the overflow of delight celebrating Jesus as God's blessing.[22]

Joy as noise overflowed in oral cultures where learning the faith as well as praise required the public reading of Scripture, teaching and song. The communal character of faith in ancient oral cultures privileged sound. This is why Ambrose of Milan was regarded with suspicion when he read silently. Only with the arrival of the printing press in 1440s and a rise in urban literacy did reading and praying in silence become possible for many people outside the cloisters of the Monastery. Even so, word centred Protestant preaching continued to ensure that sound was a key expression of faith even though music was often seen as suspect because of its seductive power. In addition the Book of Common Prayer and the King James Bible were appointed for public reading whilst Richard Hooker believed that public prayer was more trustworthy than solitary prayer because a shared understanding of Scripture was less likely to be mistaken than a singular one. Later revivals, such as nineteenth-century Methodism and the nineteenth-century Evangelical and Oxford Revivals were all characterised by noise whilst Pentecostal Gospel singing and charismatic worship ensured that noisy spirituality was embedded within mainstream Christianity.[23]

HUMANS AND SOUND

Sound is also significant for Christian spirituality because intelligible noise, music and speech are key marks of being human. To be human is to be a linguistic music making animal, a singing, speaking project, which David Ford calls the 'singing self'.[24] We are naming creatures who give meaning to things and events through language. We are culture forming creatures mediating our learning and memory through language and music. We are social creatures whose language enables us to participate in society and speak with God conversationally. We are story creatures who narrate our lives in order to find meaning in them. We are freedom-seeking creatures who through language rise above mere existence to contemplate ourselves in time and place. This is why sound, particularly the intelligible sound of language, is so important for life in the Spirit. It shows that we are made in the image of God whose words respond to the Word spoken in Jesus.

LIFE IN THE SPIRIT AND SIGHT

I had to give up playing rugby in my mid-twenties because my eyeballs increasingly took on the shape of rugby balls and I became too short sighted to see the opposition, let alone the ball. At least cycling can be done wearing glasses. Short sightedness though has made me very aware of the preciousness of having good sight and explains why I believe that cultivating good spiritual sight is important in the Christian life since it enables us to see the truth about God, a bit like an artist seeking to see the truth of the material world.[25] And like artists we come to see beauty, love and truth through pain and suffering because they prevent our life in the Spirit being simply a form of self-deception and fantasy. Seeing truthfully is not easy in the spiritual life and we need to be trained to see with integrity and virtue.[26] This tough training takes time and involves learning the language and traditions of the Christian community if we are to see the truth and goodness of God in the world more fully.

BIBLE AND SIGHT

In the first creation story light is the first created reality.[27] Without light there can be no sight since we can only see because of an already existing radiance. In the first chapter of Genesis light is present before the creation of sun and moon as a reminder that the source of light and therefore the capacity for sight is God. As Psalm 119:130 indicates, 'the unfolding of your words gives light. It imparts understanding to the simple.' This light is explored in subsequent texts and is identified as Torah and Wisdom. In Proverbs 6:23, 'the commandment is a lamp and the teaching a light, and the reproofs of discipline are the way of life' while Psalm 36:9 proclaims that 'with you is the fountain of life; in your light do we see light' and Psalm 34:8 invites listeners to 'taste and see that the Lord is good'. The impact of this light is evident in the role of seers, such as Samuel, who see divine activity in the midst of Israel's life. Yet as the story of the burning bush shows us this divine light does not destroy the world but rather respects its integrity.[28] It is light that attracts our attention to God's truth rather than imposing it upon us.[29]

According to Gordon Mursell, the Fourth Gospel gives us a rich meditation on light and sight.[30] The Prologue is a midrash or meditative commentary on Genesis 1 identifying Jesus with the Logos of creation whose life is light.[31] As light, Christ enables believers to see since in him the divine radiance continues to shine, is stronger than darkness and is entering the world. This light invites moral choice, a choice Judas makes negatively when his betrayal is marked by the phrase 'it was night'.[32] The judgement of Jesus as light of the world is expressed though his ministry as Messiah and especially in his death which is his glory.[33] To see Jesus as light is therefore to believe in who he is and what he reveals of God. It is to be transformed by what we see of the fullness of God in the glory of the cross.[34] Nicodemus is therefore the representative disciple who begins in the dark but ends in the light.[35] Yet in this light the Fourth Gospel opens up a range of insights about sight and the spiritual life. The Gospel is presented as a court case in which Jesus and his adversaries are being tried. Witnesses are those who testify of what they have seen and this is why the writer wrote this Gospel.[36] John the Baptist is also a witness to the Messiah who challenges his listeners to 'behold (or see) the Lamb of God'.[37]

DISCIPLESHIP AND SIGHT

For Rowan Williams, being disciples involves staying with Jesus so that we come to see what he is up to. We must become students of Jesus which, in the ancient world meant 'to commit yourself to living in the same atmosphere and breathing the same air'.[38] This hanging around with Jesus involves watching what he does and says so that we come to see the world differently. For the Fourth Gospel this is a cumulative process in which we learn to see the meaning of Christ through the seven signs of this Gospel. Jesus invites the disciples to come and hang around with him so that they will see.[39] The disciples then invite others such as Philip and Nathaniel to hang around Jesus.[40] This sharing of life is how they and we come to

ON YOUR BIKE

see the Messiah as the new Jacob's ladder joining heaven and earth, a sight the Greek pilgrims seek when they say 'Sir we would see Jesus!'[41] It involves walking in the light and believing in the light just as the disciple whom Jesus loved, the archetype for all Christians, sees and believes rather than simply sees when he enters the empty tomb.[42] In this way the Spirit leads people into all truth so that they come to see the rich meaning of Jesus clearly, particularly when they believe when they can no longer see Jesus in the flesh.[43]

Other New Testament writings echo these themes. Witnessing is key to Acts, whilst living in the light is a central theme of Paul's writings and also of the Letters of John. In Luke's story of the Walk to Emmaus, seeing means understanding who Jesus is. The two disciples recognise or see Jesus in the breaking of the bread.[44] According to Roger Walton each Gospel sees the impact of Jesus distinctively.[45] For Mark, seeing Jesus is about mission: 'Come and follow me and I will make you fishers of people.'[46] For Luke, seeing Jesus is about worship: 'and they were continually in the Temple praising God.'[47] For John, seeing Jesus is about community: 'a new commandment I give to you to love one another as I have loved you.'[48] For Matthew, seeing Jesus is about education: 'every scribe who has been trained for the kingdom of heaven is like a householder who brings out of his treasure what is new and what is old.'[49]

FAITH AND SIGHT

So mission, worship, community and learning belong together in Christian spirituality since it is as we learn to see Jesus in the performance of his mission (seeking him in Galilee), in worship (the breaking of the bread), in community (the practice of loving strangers) and in learning (discipleship formation), that we grasp the truth of his identity more fully and can witness more authentically in this world. As we become communities, through forgiveness, of restored relationships we become able to discern the truth of God in the world.[50] Forgiveness therefore enables us to see the world as sacramental, a sign of God's activity, rather than simply as a utility to be exploited since in the world's magnificent complexity we see the bright mystery of God.[51] Forgiveness also speaks of facing each other in love since seeing the face shows us the irreplaceable uniqueness of the other and underlies the importance of human dignity. As the Jewish philosopher Levinas realised when in the Nazi death camps, refusal to see the face made the horrors of the Holocaust possible as people were collectivised into faceless selves. Furthermore, Christians also believe that we are faced by Jesus as well as facing Jesus and so live in the gaze of his love.[52]

A spirituality of sight, therefore. is about being drawn to the radiance of God just as Moses was drawn to the burning bush. We come to see the ways of God truthfully as we listen to Scripture within the community of the Church as that ongoing conversing, performing and witnessing sign of God's mission in the world. This spirituality invites us to 'come and see where Jesus is staying!' It refuses the self-referential seeing of celebrity culture in which being seen or noticed is everything.[53] Instead it seeks sainthood so that others can see the light of God, the burning bush of love, through lives dedicated to God's service. It sees the uniqueness of each particular element of creation with virgin eyes and, like a child, looks with wonder and awe at the gift of life and of salvation 'softening how we look and seeing with a wider angle' in worship and contemplation.[54]

ON YOUR BIKE

LIFE IN THE SPIRIT AND SIGNS

We live in a sign culture, yet it is difficult is to recognise truthful signs in a society of strangers. We also live in a culture hostile to hypocrisy and in favour of sincerity. Yet sincerity can simply be unjustified assertion. Both of these cultural trends are magnified by the internet which presents us with surface people and no means to test their character. As a result, all sorts of fundamentalisms flourish since fundamentalism is a modern form of impatience with the complexity of truth. It is surface spirituality seeking an escape from contingency and history. We can see this in the rise of Islamist fundamentalism in which disaffected men and women, with criminality in their background and little education or understanding of the Qu'ran, are presented as exemplars of sacrificial sincerity. The violence of their deaths is stitched into a story of high moral virtue and purpose as a shortcut to sainthood. Yet this notion that sincerity is all that matters has also been fed by our politicians, our economics, by celebrity and by sections of the media. Their stress on personal autonomy and freedom from the constraints of time, place and history has undermined the sense that we are all 'somewhere people', located in relationships and places which enable us to be known.[55] Indeed many people now appear unrooted and simply preoccupied with cash, convenience and consumerism. According to sociologist Zygmunt Bauman late modern societies form people into 'decadent vagabonds' living the slogan 'I am, I want, I will'. As a result, claims to sincerity are all that is left.[56] Yet the incarnation shows us that Christian spirituality is about life together in the Spirit in the material world. It is faith in flesh, God's sign to a world in flight from the embodied and situated. This faith in flesh is the Church, a tangible, social sign which points to the promise that God will reign on earth as in heaven.

IN THE SPIRIT

BIBLE AND SIGN

The idea of life with God as a social sign has its roots in Israel's call to social holiness. Israel's covenant with the Lord was about being holy as the Lord is holy in a visible and material way.[57] It was lived holiness in a land which spoke of place, gift, promise and challenge.[58] It was life ordered by detailed Torah injunctions and Wisdom guidance held to account by prophetic challenge and focused for much of its history on a Temple which signed the meeting of heaven and earth. Israel was called to be a light to the nations and within this vocation emerged an understanding of the goodness of creation which, unlike contemporary paganism, was not identical with God or a divine spirit but identified with God and God's character.[59] This situated, social holiness manifested itself in worship expressed through touch, taste and smell. The three major Festivals of Passover, Pentecost and Tabernacles were tangible dramas of recollection involving eating, feeling and smell. Liturgy, as we noted, was noisy and dramatically mapped Israel's memory and sense of time. The Torah which began as torahs, the spiritual guidance of priests, grew to represent the revelation of Yahweh to Israel. This was later written up as a more formal record of Israel's story in the sixth century BC during the Babylonian Exile. These writings gave detailed insights into the practices which displayed love of God and love of neighbour through the lens of justice and righteousness exemplified in care of the marginalised and the powerless represented by the orphan, widow and stranger. The very material character of this shared life meant that sin was also a tangible reality which needed material resolution in the form of sacrifice. Hence the sacrificial practices focussed on the Temple and the economy which this generated. Yet this enfleshed spirituality was not an end

ON YOUR BIKE

in itself. Its goal was to form a people of public holiness. As we read in Hosea, the Lord says, 'I desire steadfast love and not sacrifice, the knowledge of God rather than burnt offerings.'[60]

In the New Testament Jesus was the sign of this material spirituality par excellence. He was the true Israelite. John calls him the Word of God enfleshed and Matthew calls him Emmanuel, God-with-us. Paul speaks of him as the icon of God within whom the fullness of God dwells and who accommodated himself to the limitations of creation in order to embody love and rescue humankind from the judgement of sin.[61] This is the story of God present within creation as a Jewish man of the first century in Palestine. This is where he stays and where God's glory or self-disclosure is seen in his death.[62] Consequently Christians are called to follow the risen Jesus into ordinary life, our Galilee, shaped by this story of glory and the practical wisdom of discipleship. This is why Paul speaks about having the mind or practical intelligence of Christ Jesus.[63] Furthermore, Jesus is raised to a new yet material life in which his sacrificed body is now present in the sacraments of his community. 'Unless you eat the flesh of the Son of Man and drink his blood you have no life within you'.[64] As St Paul says, the Church is the Body of Christ, a fleshly sign of the new creation, worshipping Christ and witnessing to the Reign of God which is characterised by the remarkable hospitality of Pentecost.[65] It is also now a community for all people and places, a conviction which emerged as the impact of Pentecost led to the conversion of Gentiles and thereby ensured that the Jesus sect became a global movement. God's Spirit meets people where they are in the culture and languages they inhabit and speak.[66]

IN THE SPIRIT

CHURCH AND SIGN

As a result, the social sign of the Church was one of the most powerful evangelistic signs of the Gospel and life in the Spirit. As we saw in chapter 5, this Christian *ekklesia,* the Christian Citizens' Assembly, transformed Hellenistic and Jewish cultural modes of belonging. The Church was the sign of the impact of Christ on humankind seen in an inclusive rather than segregated community. In contrast the Greek *ekklesia* was restricted to free men and the Jewish Synagogue was led by male Jews, with a segregated section reserved for women on a balcony or sometimes in a separate building. The early Church through Baptism included free and slave, male and female, child and adult, poor and rich in one community in one place.[67] It was a sign of God's universal community in which those without citizenship were welcomed as citizens of heaven.[68] Here was a home for the homeless and a society for all people. Indeed, as Rowan Williams argues, it was the existence of a church of all people which Athanasius used to defeat the arguments of Arius in their third century debate about the divinity of Christ, since only God could save all.[69] Such convictions underlie the hostility of early Christians to the Gnostics who sought to escape the limitations and corruption of the body since Christians believed that the revelation of God was in the flesh. As we have seen, this was at the heart of Augustine of Hippo's contest with the Donatists and Manichees. The former's perfectionist spirituality sought to escape timebound, finite and fallen existence whereas the latter's regarded the body as an evil constraint on true spirituality. Both were a refusal to live within the realities of creation, fallenness and incarnation, and refused to believe that as the incarnate one 'God has placed himself in the order of signs'.[70] Fleshly spirituality also shaped the monastic movement from its earliest days since monks lived together in disciplined communities in the hope of communal sanctification. The monastery sought to be a sign of love in which loving the other or the stranger was very tangible. Touch, taste and smell were daily realities of life at such close quarters as monks and nuns learned how to love the real brother or sister in their communities. This was also why they refused to flee from the community when the loving got tough because they were a pledged community who stayed together in the struggle of life and faced themselves and one another in a very tangible way.[71]

Life in the Spirit therefore is life with others in worship, witness and blessing within the communities and places where we live, work and serve.[72] Place matters especially to the poor who are often placed and therefore unable to move or choose in the way the affluent can and so the Church also needs to be rooted among such communities. For Davison and Milbank this is a challenge to forms of Christian belonging which sit lightly to context and situation.[73] It is also why Stanley Hauerwas roots ethics in community life since it is in the practices of liturgy and service that we are formed into an embodied apologetic of the Gospel.[74] Life in the Spirit is therefore about living with Christ as creatures in time and place aware that 'to be an intelligence in time is to be inescapably unfinished, constantly in search.'[75] Such a spirituality reminds us of our incompleteness and is not an escape from living in time but is about discovering God within our time. It is holiness in finitude since 'God's rhetoric is no argument but fleshly life', fleshly life which bears the marks of its Creator.[76]

CONCLUSION

The Church is a public community with dual citizenship of earth and heaven. It is a 'movement directed by and to the holiness of God' which seeks to face God and become

IN THE SPIRIT

a sign of social holiness pointing to the destiny of all in God.[77] Anglicanism seeks to reflect this in its historical approach to understanding faith. For Anglicans the Church is a history of God's activity in which the gift of God in Jesus Christ is embodied in worship, wisdom and service in contextually sensitive mission which seeks the common good for all.[78] Life in the Spirit is therefore a holy spirituality in which our bodies are inspired with the life of God. It is about faith in flesh rather than faith escaping flesh. This is a spirituality of the senses in which silence, sound, sight and sign express and enrich our relationship with God. The Church is that community open to the Spirit in which we learn how to explore our journey into the depths of God's love in this world. It is precisely as we face the reality of each other, our differences and our failings as well as our joys and passions, that we discover the Spirit as that love which makes strangers into friends of God and one another.

Questions for reflection

1. How does silence enrich your devotional life?
2. What sorts of sound enable you to worship most fully?
3. In what ways has serving Christ shaped your view of life?
4. What sort of sign of the Gospel does your local church represent?

CHAPTER 8
In the Rough

ROUGH RIDES

I don't ride in the rough much these days. However, I do enjoy occasional off-road escapades and in the past have cycled coastal paths, crossed fords, peddled dirt tracks and used the Sustrans Cycle routes to test my modest mettle. As a child I saw lots of cyclists coping with dirt and rutted roads in Uganda, carrying remarkable loads with apparently carefree abandon. I learned too of faithful pastors cycling long distances to far-flung congregations in areas where foot and car were either too slow or impossible. In addition, what I have most enjoyed about off-road riding is the opportunity to explore creation in ways tarmac roads limit. It has exposed me to the drama of nature through the year and enabled me to see the detail of the countryside. Riders like Mark Beaumont whose book *The Man Who Cycled the World* relates the story of his record-breaking ride, inspire awe and wonder, as well as giving readers a vicarious experience of the globe.[1] I am not this sort of cyclist. However since different riders have different capacities and interests, riding in the rough will mean different things to different people. What riding in the rough exposes for all cyclists is the vulnerability of riders as they engage with the challenges of different terrain and conditions. Riding in the rough also gives one a profound respect for bikes.

IN THE ROUGH

They may look insubstantial but actually demonstrate huge resilience in the demands of this sort of riding.

Being a follower of Jesus Christ in the contemporary western world can feel like riding in the rough. Religious illiteracy among the chattering classes makes for tiresome listening as simplistic, superficial dismissal shuts down serious engagement with the questions which religions and in particular Christianity raise. There is an assumption that God is a projection based upon our immature needs and so to be free is to be liberated from this dependency. Equally this god is seen as a rival whose overwhelming power means that human beings have no freedom. This fear leads to a focus on the ideals of human autonomy, freedom and choice even though most of the human race have little experience of these due to poverty and abusive political systems. Yet increasingly artificial intelligence, technology and media increasingly undermine these ideals as elites control more and more of life and thereby threaten human agency and value as Shoshana Zuboff has argued.[2] Furthermore the COVID-19 pandemic has also disrupted this story of freedom, choice and autonomy as lockdowns, restrictions and dependency have come to the fore and the inequalities in our society laid bare. Indeed, as David Goodhart has indicated, this disruption has also led to a re-evaluation of social value as roles which benefited from this narrative, which he calls head roles, have been seen to be less significant than those roles which he calls hand and heart roles, traditionally associated with place, people and stability. An example of such re-evaluation is the way public service workers and health workers have been the heroes of the COVID pandemic. Furthermore, the destruction of the Twin Towers in New York on 11 September 2001 by Islamic extremist network al-Qaeda challenged the idea that modernisation would lead to secularisation and the decline of religion.

ON YOUR BIKE

While this horrific action in no way reflected the dominant traditions of Islam, it showed that religion, as an inspiration and world-view, was alive and active in much of the world. Indeed about 85 per cent of the global population subscribe to a religious faith making western secularism an exceptional and minority view unlikely to win world dominance. In particular, Christianity and Islam are growing across the world and their demographic is getting younger and less Euro or American-centric. So globally religious belief is not going to disappear even if, in the West, sceptical secularism has made significant inroads into popular thinking. The challenge for Christian ministers and thinkers in this secularist environment is to show how Christianity continues to engage fruitfully, creatively and persuasively with the difficult questions of our society. In the next section I grapple with three such questions: the first about truth, the second about sex and the third about the climate emergency. Each of these debates is complex and contested and all I can do is share where I have got to in these conversations and how I have approached them as a conversation with Scripture, tradition and sound learning or reasoning. This means that I welcome more persuasive arguments to challenge my own and help me see more clearly. Indeed as an Anglican committed to synodical process I want to walk with those who disagree with me as well as with those who feel closer to the positions which I outline. In this way a clearer grasp of the truth we are seeking can emerge as we engage together with Scripture, tradition and sound learning. This approach is never finished since we live in time. It therefore seeks provisional settlements which can be revised in the face of new insights and interpretations of Scripture. Nevertheless the process represents a commitment to seeking the best truth we can since we are ultimately accountable to God in whom is all truth.

IN THE ROUGH

TRUTH
Truth and today

The election in 2016 of Donald Trump, the Brexit vote and the rise of popularism and fake news exposed a contest about truth in the western world, putting truth and power in tension.[3] Evidence-based claims were challenged on the grounds that these apparently innocent claims actually represented bids for power by elites who had diminished and marginalised ordinary people, their traditions, perspectives and identities which contributed to a collapse in trust.[4] Yet 'a world of truth is a world of trust' and without the one it is impossible to have the other.[5] Ironically it was the very abuse of trust which opened up this contest since contemporary scepticism is but the political manifestation of some post-modern approaches to truth in the wake of the totalitarian ideologies of the twentieth century, such as Fascism and Communism which claimed to have a total and universally objective vision of life. Such claims draw strength from nineteenth-century Positivism. Positivism is the belief that we can grasp truth in a way that excludes perspective and interests and in a way which corresponds to reality. Positivism is present whenever someone separates subject and object and assumes that the latter can be known by the former as it really is.

Post modernity was a reaction against the abuses and deceptions of this philosophical approach rightly noting that human beings are limited, situated and understand or explain life as contingent beings. We live in space and time. This means that we are implicated in the process of knowing and have no objective access to what is true. We cannot therefore achieve a total or universal view of anything. Even the so-called hard truths of the natural sciences are the best hypotheses so far for what scientists regard as the evidence appropriate to their field of research. These hypotheses are constantly being tested and if found to be inadequate (falsified) are changed to take account of new insights. In the humanities such as History, English and Languages, which explore the human as subject, explanation through experiment and observation is not enough. To understand other human beings we need to listen to what they tell us rather than simply observing them. This will involve interpreting what they say through speech and text to see how plausible and persuasive it is. To reach towards the truth in this way does not mean that there is no objective world or that truth is simply assertion. The very fact that scientific hypotheses are forced to change as the evidence they are based upon changes, that we adapt our language in response to new realities and that unsought out experiences such as the beauty of art or the agony of suffering impact upon us, shows this. However, even though we find ourselves changing our minds, we do so as those involved in making sense of that change and of how it is understood. Truth therefore is complex and multi-faceted and is relative to the field of inquiry under question.[6] Our grasp of truth is therefore always an approximation rather than a possession. We are on a journey towards the truth rather than having arrived.

TRUTH AND THE BIBLE

Both the Old and New Testaments are concerned with truth. In John's Gospel Jesus is 'the way, the truth and the life', that is the one who reveals the truth about the Father and the way to eternal life.[7] In the wisdom and prophetic traditions truth is expressed as faithfulness, firmness of purpose, trustworthiness and reliability. This understanding of truth is about the tangible rather than the abstract, deeds rather than ideas. It is a pragmatic and moral understanding of truth rather than a speculative view, which explains why hypocrisy is seen by Jesus as such a serious sin. Truth in the Bible is also about seeking the closest correspondence with reality as well as about coherence and performance, so Christians have a stake in the quest for the empirical because of our conviction that God has created a universe which is coherent and can be meaningfully investigated and is intelligible. This is the also an implication of the opening verses of the Prologue of the Fourth Gospel where the Word, who is identified as Jesus, is the self-expression of God and shows us that at the heart of God is a longing to speak, relate and communicate.

TRUTH AND CHRISTIANITY

Christians therefore understand truth to be rational and evidence-based, which explains why contemporary science and hermeneutics emerged from within the Christian tradition. Furthermore, Christians believe that creation has its own integrity which is sustained and permeated by the grace of God. Consequently creation is identified with but is not identical to its Creator and so science and the humanities explore the range and depth of God's handiwork without being trumped by a privileged theocratic approach to knowledge. This is what Christians mean by a secular approach to a rational and coherent creation and it was this which provided the incentive for exploring the cosmos in a secular way not seen in the classical world. As Larry Siedentop argues, 'properly understood, secularism can be seen as Europe's noblest achievement, the achievement which should be its primary contribution to the creation of a world order ... secularism is Christianity's gift to the world, ideas and practices which have often been turned against "excesses" of the Christian Church itself.'[8] The eighteenth-century Enlightenment, which became associated with secularisation and the rejection of theology, actually depended upon these Christian insights and early modern scientists such as Galileo and Bacon were not in conflict with Christianity because they were Christians. Rather their battle was with conservative clergy.

Christianity therefore underwrites the modern quest for truth in all its many forms convinced that its unity and coherence are founded in God and will ultimately find their unity in God. This is why Christians believe in universities rather than multi-versities. Western liberalism and the pursuit of truth are the offspring of the Christian faith, which not only encouraged the empirical method in the sciences, but also ensured that in seeking the truth the humanities explored the whole of humanity rather than simply the world of elites.

SEX
A North-South divide
Debates about sexuality have become the new frontier of conflict between traditionalists, who claim to be faithful to the historical tradition, and those they call revisionists. Revisionists are seen as changing that tradition in order to make it compatible with contemporary western norms that conflict with traditional views. For Anglicans this argument has a political dimension since the largest concentration of Anglicans is in the Global South. Broadly these Anglicans take a traditionalist line whereas the advocates of revision are predominantly in the Global North whose thinking has been shaped by the eighteenth-century Enlightenment and its critical view of tradition. Arguments about sexuality are therefore a proxy for Church politics as the large and growing churches in the Global South assert their claim to represent and determine the Anglican Communion's response to questions of sex and sexuality. Secondly these arguments are a response to the challenge of Islam in sub-Saharan Africa where Islam can represent itself as a simple, pure faith in one God, one Holy Book and one Prophet which together give followers clear instructions about holy living. These

laws can seem closer to traditional African convictions and, despite the history of Islamic slave trading and conquest, are often unfairly presented as free from the colonialism associated with Christianity. Thirdly these arguments must be seen within the context of inter-Christian rivalry in the Global South. African Independent Churches challenge Anglican African churches because they synthesize traditional African religion and Christianity in ways that appeal to many Africans.[9] Pentecostalism threatens Anglicans with its mix of fundamentalism and lively, expressive worship. Lastly it seems that some rich conservative Episcopalians from the Southern States of the United States of America see this issue as part of an ongoing culture war between themselves and the more liberal northern states which has not been resolved since the nineteenth-century American Civil War.

As someone formed in both the Global South and North I am torn by this conflict. I believe that recent scientific, anthropological and historical research shows us that sex and gender can no longer be seen in the simple binary way of our ancestors.[10] Yet I love the African Church which formed me and has inspired my faith and ministry. As a consequence, when I listen to Christians in the Global South, to feminist thinkers and to sexual minorities such as LGBTQ+ communities, I am caught between their perspectives. I try to understand their different interpretations on the Bible and the Christian Tradition, frustrated that the issues are oversimplified by those at the extremes of the debate. As someone who has lived in the Global North and South I also know that Christians in the Global South have been formed very differently from those in the North. For example the Global North is present and future focussed, whereas the Global South has a deep respect for the past and is therefore reserved about changes to established belief and practice. Hence in much of Africa there is a reluctance to break with the ancestors' wisdom in contrast to the Global North which sees its liberation as freedom, from the limitations and shackles of the past. All this means that change is regarded positively in the Global North whereas continuity is seen as positive in the Global South.

The pressure to change emerging from the Global North is a further cause of sensitivity since to the Global South this feels like another expression of colonialism which disrupts and disturbs their societies. In the Global North there is still little acknowledgement of our historic impact on the Global South and on the whole we assume that our view of change is good for all people. Of course societies in the Global South are not all the same. South Africa is very different to Uganda as a result of the struggle against apartheid and the intellectual and social resources that were drawn upon to engage in that struggle. Consequently South Africa has been more sensitive about oppression of any kind, sexual or other. So inter-African argument further contributes to suspicions, which subvert trust and lead traditionalists to use the issue as a litmus test for orthodoxy. In such an atmosphere it is difficult to know whether mutual understanding is possible or even desired. In what follows I try to offer a way of framing the issues which might lead to some sort of rapprochement.

The Bible and sex

A cursory reading of the Old Testament suggests that whilst these Scriptures testify to human dignity in the language of equality and worth, Israel understood gender and sexual attraction as simple and binary based upon observation of physical anatomy. This determined what was natural and unnatural. Hence, although passages such as the story of Sodom in Genesis 18 v. 26--19 v.29, the two passages from Leviticus which prohibit sex between men and the one in Deuteronomy 23 vv. 17--18 can be shown to be about rape, prostitution or are embedded in lists of commands which are no longer observed (such as wearing mixed threaded clothing or killing people for Sabbath breaking), it was assumed that sexual activity was properly between male and female given the anatomical differences and the imperative of reproduction to ensure the people's survival. To depart from this reproductive responsibility was an act of selfishness which put at risk the future of the tribe, as well as dishonouring the holiness God sought in his people. In modern language such behaviour also made one a free rider imposing costs on the community in terms of welfare in sickness and old age since one had no children to act as carers. Marriage therefore was a way of ordering this reproduction responsibly to secure a safe future for the tribe and its children whilst offering relative social and economic security to men and women. Companionship might be present in marriages, but for most ancient societies including Israel this was not the determining factor in the relationship, which was fundamentally about reproduction and social identity. The lifelong character of marriage, whether monogamous or polygamous, reflected the indivisible union of their one flesh embodied in their offspring and was modelled on God's covenant faithfulness with his special people Israel. This also explains why Israel was so hostile to pagan fertility cults and their sexual practices.

If we look at the way Jesus and the early Church interacted with this tradition, we see that as a faithful, first-century Jew, Jesus was obedient to the Torah. Yet his status as a single man, his comments on eunuchs, his silence on same-sex relationship, his assertion that marriage will not be part of the fullness of the Kingdom of God, and his prioritising of the disciple community above the biological family showed that an obedient life need not include the duty of biological reproduction. This transcending of the biological imperative can also be seen in Paul who was also single, perhaps widowed, yet found this gave him freedom to proclaim the Gospel across the known world. Furthermore, Jesus' band of disciples was gender mixed and he himself engaged in taboo breaking conversations which challenged accepted gender norms. For example the Nazareth Manifesto in Luke Chapter 4 envisaged a new era community in which the most excluded were included. His summary of Torah faithfulness as 'love God wholeheartedly and love neighbour as self' or in John's tradition 'love one another as I have loved you' gave shape to the character of this new community. His commitment to forgiveness and loving strangers such as those whose morals, race, gender, infertility and age set them outside the boundaries of Jewish acceptability provided a further challenge to inherited assumptions.

Jesus was less concerned about pure social identity and more about God's welcome and redemption, particularly of those who suffered from the abuse of power. This did not mean that inclusiveness had no boundaries. However, the boundaries he rejected were ones set up by those closed to forgiveness and love for the stranger. Consequently in the Early Church, baptism and Eucharist, dramatic signs of the Gospel, demonstrated that God's new community was for all people. Indeed this inclusive Church was radically evangelistic as it contrasted with the stratified and unequal social order of Jewish and Greco-Roman societies. The debate about boundaries in Acts Chapter 15 shows an improvising approach to inclusion in which generous hospitality was more important than social and legal purity within the new age of the Spirit. The story of Jesus, which included socially challenging approaches to friendships between and within genders, races, economic classes and ages, gestured to an improvising faith seeking to follow the Spirit in the pursuit of unfolding truth as new insights emerge which question the adequacy of earlier assumptions. It is this story which provides the lens and trajectory through which to interpret and improvise upon the inherited Scriptures.

The Church and sex

We can see such improvisation throughout Church History. For example, when the fourth-century Constantinian Settlement established Christianity as the religion of the Roman Empire communities which sought a life of single-minded faithfulness they went into the desert to form single sex monastic communities of prayer devoted to spiritual rather than biological reproduction in a way quite unusual in Judaism. Monastic communities spread all over the Greco-Roman world as ordered communities of lifelong vowed commitment characterised by poverty, chastity and obedience. This friendship with God and one another was very different to Greco-Roman assumptions about friendship. In contrast to Cicero's view, that to meet a friend is to look into a mirror, these vowed communities required that monks learned how to love the stranger represented by their fellow monks. A further example of change in the tradition took place with the invention of the printing press. This enabled large and cumbersome manuscripts to be printed as one text at a time and also coincided with greater awareness of Islam, with its rival, single revelatory text. The impact of both the printing press and Islam changed the way the Bible was seen, particularly in Protestant communities. Increasingly the Bible was seen as a single, unified text, which could be read by anyone anywhere rather than a series of diverse texts to be read in a liturgical context. The portable Bible enabled the emergence of fundamentalist, surface ways of reading the text as a simple, singular and timeless source of information about God and God's ways with the world.

ON YOUR BIKE

Such approaches to the Bible were contested. For example the sixteenth-century Elizabethan theologian, Richard Hooker, believed that this way of reading the Bible was simplistic. He argued that public reading of Scripture was always more trustworthy than private reading of Scripture since the complexity of the texts needed training in exegetical skills, not simple literacy. For Hooker, a Puritan approach to reading Scripture flattened out the Bible with every part having equal authority. In contrast he believed it should be read through the lens of the story of Jesus Christ within the context of particular cultures. Consequently some doctrinal change could happen in response to new challenges to inherited practice and custom within different cultures. An example of this was John Calvin's view that lending money at interest to other Christians was not always sinful because borrowing and lending were now seen as mutually beneficial, so long as the risk was equally shared. This was in sharp contrast to the Medieval Church's hostility to usury within the Christian community. In the nineteenth century, slavery also came to be seen as immoral and counter to Christian notions of human dignity while in the twentieth century the Church of England accepted contraception and broke the link between heterosexual intercourse and reproduction. Accepting contraception meant recognising that most sexual activity was now primarily recreational and about deepening companionship rather than principally reproductive as in the past. Finally same-sex attraction became medicalised in the nineteenth century and labelled homosexuality in contrast to heterosexuality, a description unknown to the biblical world. Despite all attempts to 'turn' homosexual people into heterosexuals, the science increasingly agreed that this was neither possible nor desirable and the mainline Churches have publicly come out against such practices. Indeed in the first half of the twentieth century the Church of England was at the forefront of the campaign to decriminalise sexual activity between consenting same-sex adults even though it regarded this activity as sinful. Same-sex attraction was now increasingly seen as normal and natural for those involved rather than a perversion. This change in understanding changed the moral landscape and has led to demands for civil and religious equality by sexual minorities akin to those of liberation struggles over race, gender and colonialism. It is this changed understanding of sexuality and gender and the moral implications of this change which have led many Christians to revise their traditional understanding, just as their faith ancestors revised their understanding of Gentiles, women, money and slavery.[11] This is not about undermining Scripture and tradition but recognising that they are testimony to an ongoing and unfolding relationship with God and reality in which new truths based upon sound learning emerge.[12] This has been the case in debates about gender and race and I believe should happen in other areas of life including sexuality.[13]

Marriage, companionship and sex

Since the sixteenth-century Reformation, the institution of marriage as understood by the Church of England has three purposes: reproduction, fidelity and companionship. Marriage signs the creative, faithful and relationship between Christ and the Church and also involves loving the most vulnerable neighbour, the possible child, who is the potential outcome of every fertile act of sexual union by the two adults involved. In addition marriage is a sign of the role of a particular male and female in a child's conception, it clarifies the identity of the child and reminds the biological parents that they have responsibilities for its formation. Other modes of reproduction involve a third

ON YOUR BIKE

party and thereby complicate the identity of the child and loosen the responsibility of the biological parents even though there are examples of surrogacy in the Old Testament. So whilst adoption enables those who cannot reproduce to nurture a child whose own biological parents are unable to do so, this is a remedial act akin to God's adoption of us through baptism.

Christians have therefore regarded the sign of reproduction as a key part of the institution of marriage along with companionship and faithful intimacy, whether a particular marriage has offspring or not. Marriage has been seen as the institution which enables responsible reproduction and ensures that children have an identifiable heritage. Indeed it is arguable that this is why marriage should be a lifelong commitment since the growing child bodily represents their union unfolding. Recent equal marriage legislation in the United Kingdom has removed reproduction from the purposes of civil marriage in order to accommodate same-sex marriages to demonstrate equal respect for equally natural relationships. Civil marriage is now the vowed lifelong commitment by two individuals of any sexual orientation without any formal link with reproduction. In the light of new and evidence-based insights about human sexuality many Anglicans now recognise that same-sex attraction is natural for those who experience it. Indeed there are many committed same-sex relationships, which like marriage, embody companionship and faithful intimacy even though they are not in themselves biologically reproductive. As such they embody key virtues which matter to Christians. Such committed companionship has affinities with that of monastic orders. In a world in which contraception is available and where reproductive sex is no longer necessary for all, such companionship and intimate sexual behaviour are no longer a threat to society.

IN THE ROUGH

Conclusion

The Church of England continues to teach that Christian marriage is a covenant between a man and a woman because of its theological significance and because it signs the necessary conditions for companionship, sexual fidelity and new biological life. Priests therefore bless marriages because they include this reproductive, theologically important sign even if particular couples are beyond fertile years or cannot themselves have children. This, though, does not imply that other expressions of faithful companionship cannot be blessed or accorded equal respect. For example monastic vows are blessed and dignified as a sign of commitment and fidelity to God lived out in same-sex communities of companions whose purpose is spiritual rather than biological reproduction. In the light of the above and with the more expansive understanding we now have of same-sex relationships, I believe that committed and faithful same-sex relationships should also be accorded public recognition and blessing by the Church in a way which acknowledges their virtues, distinctiveness and equal value. As D. Stephen Long says 'we are attempting to make space for persons made in the image of God who have been silenced and marginalised for centuries and whose natural desires, orientations and biological realities need sanctifying grace.'[14]

Some also argue further that since same-sex attraction is natural for some in society and the primacy of reproduction is no longer the defining characteristic of a fulfilled marriage, the institution can expand to accommodate same-sex couples in a way that guarantees public equality of dignity and respect as well as offering the security and support of an established institution. They bolster this argument by pointing to Jesus' re-positioning of marriage and biological reproduction in his teaching. Yet whilst teaching that marriage is not part of the future Kingdom and thereby relativising it, Jesus did not reject or undermine the institution of marriage in his age. Presumably this was because he saw it as the proper setting for responsible biological reproduction even though this will no longer be needed in the eternity of the Kingdom of God. So although there is a strength in this argument, especially if the institution of marriage remains the place for biological reproduction, I think more work still needs to be done within the Church about the meaning and symbolism of marriage, given the way it is used as a metaphor for Christ and the Church, and to clarify its relationship to biological reproduction.

THE CLIMATE EMERGENCY
Fracking: a case in point
In 2015 North Yorkshire became the site of a conflict between pro and anti-frackers each claiming that they were part of a green agenda. I was also aware that fracking was an issue that divided individuals, experts, commentators and communities yet as the Diocesan Ambassador for Rural Life and Faith I found myself drawn into the conflict which was focussed in the Vale of Pickering, a rural part of the Diocese. The Church of England was and is fully committed to the climate change agenda and fully supports the transition to a low-carbon economy called for by nearly 200 states at the Paris climate meeting in December 2015. Yet was fracking compatible with this commitment?[15] Part of the challenge was the character of the debate on fracking which was greatly impaired by exaggerated claims and lack of trust on both sides. On the one hand industry and the scientific community often failed to realise that their arguments were unconvincing in the affected communities. On the other hand those potentially affected by fracking appeared unwilling to engage with measured assessments of cost and benefit to society.[16] In

addition the Church of England was promoting investment in renewable energy sources and pressurising the oil and gas industry to take seriously the need to move to a low-carbon economy and had itself divested from companies specialising in the extraction of high-carbon fossil fuels such as thermal coal and oil sands. Furthermore between 2014-16 Shell, BP, Total and Statoil had agreed to enhance their reporting on operational emissions management, asset portfolio resilience against 2035 scenarios, low carbon energy research, development and investment, executive incentivisation during the low-carbon transition, and public policy activity relating to climate change. So whilst at the time the Church of England had no official policy either for or against shale gas exploration in the United Kingdom, the burden of proof lay with those promoting this form of energy extraction given the wider ecological commitments of the Church. In addition the ethical investment policy of the Church of England on climate change noted that the environmental impacts on local communities needed to be taken into account if shale gas was to be used for power generation instead of coal during the transition to a low carbon economy.

Ethics and fracking

In December 2016 the Mission and Pastoral Affairs Council (MPA) and the Environment Working Group (EWG) of the Church of England produced a briefing paper on fracking.[17] This noted the controversial character of shale gas extraction, its low public support at 17 per cent, its relatively untried character as an extraction technology in this country and stressed the importance of the government having a strategic transitional energy policy within which to situate arguments for and against fracking. The paper pointed out that only 8-20 per cent of the estimated reserves of shale gas in the United

Kingdom were potentially recoverable, that predictions about employment and economic potential were not clear and that the regulatory bodies responsible for overseeing any initiatives in this field needed to ensure that the people and environment were protected, health and safety matters adhered to and carbon emissions from fracking balanced those from other sections of the economy. In particular it stressed the importance of local people having a voice in local planning issues while also recognising that these had to be set alongside national energy security requirements and a wider conception of the Common Good. In conclusion it sought evidence-based arguments for or against fracking, pointing out that fracking was not itself morally different from any other extractive industries and that shale gas extraction in the UK was arguably cleaner than coal, oil and imported gas.

The fight about fracking

The MPA and EWG briefing paper was a careful and cautious approach in an area where vocal interest groups on both sides were vigorously promoting their perspectives without engaging with each other. So to acquaint myself with views of the respective anti and pro fracking camps I arranged two site visits. Firstly I went with a fellow Bishop to the Kirby Misperton Protection Camp which had been set up in a field near to the village to contest any attempt to frack. I then arranged an ecumenical Church leaders' visit to Third Energy at East Knapton, Malton since Third Energy wanted to frack from their gas extraction site at Kirby Misperton. In both cases there was a warm welcome, though respective positions were entrenched. The anti-fracking camp leaders argued that the government had not provided a clear energy policy to ensure that fracking would be a transitional extraction method. They feared that the set up costs would force extraction companies to see fracking as a long term investment in order to redeem the start-up costs. They pointed to the environmental damage from fracking in the United States and Australia and to the geographical and geological challenges of Yorkshire. They claimed that large scale truck movements would be needed to take contaminated water from the site and doubted that the industry had safe ways of disposing of or cleaning up this effluence. They worried about contamination of the water table, especially if there was an accident and also about the high methane emissions that would be released by the process. Given regulatory breaches elsewhere in the world, they were not persuaded by government assurances that UK regulations were gold standard. Trusting such assurances was a risky policy given the costs and challenges involved and seemed an odd approach given the low price of existing hydro-carbon energy sources which made fracking uneconomic. Furthermore tourism, local businesses and house prices would also be threatened whilst farmers' land would be at risk in any accident. Given the need to reduce CO_2 emissions by 80 per cent by 2050, subsidising fracking was short-sighted and instead the government should go all out on the green agenda.

Third Energy in contrast argued that fracking was indeed part of a transitional energy strategy and emphasized the relatively green character of locally fracked gas when compared with other gas, oil and hydrocarbon emissions from livestock. They spoke of the country's need for energy security pointing out that battery storage of power remained aspirational rather than a reality. Since 80 per cent of domestic heating and 67 per cent of cooking in the UK relied on gas the cost of adaption in the short term was also very high. They reiterated that the UK regulatory regime was very tough, that their initial frack would be exploratory and that they would need further permission from the government if longer-term fracking were to take place. They spoke of their safety record as a company and said that site visibility would be minimal so tourism should not be affected. They also argued that the Shale Wealth Fund would benefit local communities.

Conclusion

Neither of these conversations clearly indicated whether fracking was a good or a bad energy model and the briefing paper from the MPA and EWG was not prepared to use such language. Yet subsequent events and increasing evidence of climate change and the impact of fossil fuels have now stalled fracking. The challenges of Brexit negotiations, the takeover of Third Energy by the Wolfland Group, a renewable energy company, and the expansion of renewables have halted fracking in North Yorkshire even though the Chemical Company INEOS has many permits to do so and remains a potential player in the field. Furthermore the car industry is now also fully engaged in developing battery technology which bodes well for green energy storage. Christian theology speaks of the sacredness and dignity of creation as God's gift. Human beings do not own the earth which births and sustains them; they steward it on behalf of God and should do so in ways which respect its owner.[18] Given this theological vision, the urgency of climate change emergency, and our intergenerational responsibility to the unborn we cannot continue to invest in or depend upon polluting, carbon intensive fuels.[19] Fracking may indeed be a relatively cleaner form of extraction than other ways of mining fossil fuels based fuels. However to start a new fossil fuel industry in this country at this time would ignore the urgency of the situation, compete with greener solutions and work against the divine command to respect creation.

IN THE ROUGH

Questions for reflection

1. What do you find most challenging about following Christ today?
2. What does it mean to you as a Christian to be committed to the truth?
3. How would you explain your convictions about sexuality to someone with a different perspective?
4. What should your church be doing in response to the climate emergency?

CHAPTER 9
In Public

CYCLING AND THE COMMON GOOD

Cycling is a public activity. Getting on a bike for a ride takes one into public space. Sometimes this space seems empty as I used to find on my morning rides around Doncaster. At other times I found myself in contested space when sharing the road with other vehicles or with pedestrians on a cycle-pedestrian way. Sadly not all cyclists respect this public space and red lights are jumped, some cycle without lights, walkers are shaken by fast passing bikes with no bell and pavements are ridden, to the consternation of pedestrians. This is the behaviour of a minority of cyclists but it disproportionately gives cycling a bad name. However public space means space for all people rather than some and so defending the right of cyclists to share this space responsibly and in a way that respects others is equally important. Groups such as *Cycling UK* and *Sustrans* ensure that the interests of responsible cyclists are kept on the agenda of government and also offer training in good cycling practice and provide safer cycling routes. However given the relativities of power keeping those responsible for the public square focused on cyclists' needs is an ongoing challenge and is always liable to be trumped by more powerful vested interests. Ironically, the COVID-19 pandemic has given more attention to safe cycling as public transport has become less safe and segregated cycle lanes have been set up in cities and towns across the country. This has sadly led to a backlash from some motorists reminding cyclists that any public settlement is fragile and liable to be ignored when inconvenient. It is a reminder that the good life and the common good are not agreed ideas and so cyclists have to persuade society that cycling contributes to both. This is a debate about economics, law, justice, ecology and what sort of story we wish to tell about what makes for healthy living. Like religion, cycling cannot escape the challenges of power and politics and cannot risk leaving them to those who neither practise nor understand either.

Negotiating power or the business of politics therefore matters to everyone but particularly to those who feel fragile and marginal. Ministry in South Africa at the tail end of the apartheid era showed me very clearly how easily the word public can elide into elite as a powerful section of society dictates life for the rest. Hence politics needs constantly to be accountable to those affected by its decisions and, for theists, to God, our Creator and Sustainer. Otherwise it is very difficult to defend the public square from interest groups who want to colonise it for their own gain as popularist politics along with what Goodhart calls 'head' politics have revealed.[1] Politics must be accountable to those affected by the power it wields. Formally this involves elections by a universal plebiscite. However it is also about responsiveness to citizens across the social spectrum. The public square is contested space because as contingent, situated and sinful people we find it very difficult to recognise that our powerful convictions are perspectives rather than absolutes. We therefore find it difficult to empathise with others and see how our decisions impact on them. Equally, because the public square is populated with fallible people, it is necessarily a provisional space which could be different.

Many people in Britain today believe that historically a major problem has been religion as politics. Yet actually in the twentieth and twenty-first centuries the problem has been that politics has become religion. Furthermore, according to atheist philosopher John Gray, western politics is rooted in our Christian religious heritage and often hides this.[2] As Tom Holland, John Milbank, Oliver O'Donovan, Larry Siedentop, and Rowan Williams among others have shown our public space is what it is because of a long and often brutal history within which Christianity has been a key player.[3] Politics as Religion allows the penultimate to pose as the ultimate which is as dangerous as the temptation of rulers in more 'religious' ages to use God to justify their policies. The Emperors of the Roman Empire or the advocates of apartheid in South Africa are examples of this temptation. Today's public space brings with it opportunities but also challenges for Christians. Yet since God's reign is over all of life Church leaders must support the conditions for good politics while not advocating partisan policies which are necessarily divisive and represent conflicting interests in society. The short pieces which follow are a series of reflections on public life seen through the lens of Christian faith. They do not pretend to be exhaustive but try to clarify what matters as we live together in public.

THE GOOD LIFE[4]

One of my family's favourite TV shows in the 1970s was *The Good Life* because it was filmed in the suburb we lived in at the time. The drama involved Tom and Barbara Good (Richard Briers and Felicity Kendal) trying to become self-sufficient in suburban Surbiton in sharp contrast to the Leadbetters next door (Penelope Keith and Paul Eddington). This was their dream of the good life. Drama and story explore the good life as do religion and politics. Politics is about framing policies whereas religion is about forming people. In a finite, fallen and fallible world Christians accept that we won't all see eye to eye about policies. However Jesus was very clear about forming people.

IN PUBLIC

DEUTERONOMY: JUSTICE NEEDS GOOD PEOPLE.

In the Old Testament, Deuteronomy is the story of how Israel sought to live as a society exhibiting the justice of God because God's character was good and just. In an age when might was often seen as right, Israel was challenged to pursue right rather than impose might thereby ensuring justice for all people especially for the powerless. The message of Deuteronomy is that the good life is possible only as people seek to put right before might. This was what motivated the former Archbishop of York, John Sentamu as he stood up for justice against Dictator Idi Amin when he was the youngest High Court Justice in Uganda in the 1970s. He was beaten up for his troubles and eventually had to leave the country in order to save his life.

PAUL: COMMUNITY NEEDS GOOD PEOPLE.

When I was a boy in Africa we had to battle termites. You knew you had termites when you leaned against a fence post and it collapsed into dust because they had eaten it away inside out. Reading the letters of Paul we can see that a good community needs people who hold fast to what is good and love and honour others, not just themselves. Of course only God is truly good, so we seek to become good people by being rooted in God the source of goodness. In contrast bad people can't make a good society because they corrupt the political process and its goal, a challenge to societies that believe it is possible to have good politics without needing to form good people.

PUBLIC SERVICE NEEDS GOOD PEOPLE

In an age which thought greatness meant emperors, governors, generals, etc., Jesus said that greatness is about public service. It is about being the servant of all

ON YOUR BIKE

people, especially the most powerless. This is not so much about policies as about character and motivation. When the mother of disciples James and John asked Jesus to give her sons the status she felt they deserved he challenged her assumptions by saying that in his community things are done a different way. In this community good people serve rather than lord it over others and look to the needs of others before themselves.

PRAYER, POLITICS AND RELIGION[5]
Prayer means politics and religion are penultimate

Parliament began in Westminster Abbey as a form of prayerful politics and the history of the relationship between the religious and the political in English society has been one of critical friendship rather than mutual hostility. Indeed England has always prayed its politics because our ancestors believed that politics was accountable to more than itself or the popular will. Politics is ultimately accountable to God, the source and sustainer of all life, as we see in the story of the encounter between the seer Samuel and King Saul when the latter tried to fuse the political and religious in the monarchy. This was seen as contrary to the will of God and so Samuel was sent to institute political change by anointing David to be king in Saul's place.[6]

Prayer secularises religion and politics

Some people worry that religion can easily hijack politics by claiming a God's eye view of society and thereby short circuiting the political process. Given the history of conflict about religion many feel that politics should dispense with prayer. Yet politics without accountability to more than itself and the people is dangerous. The twentieth century is a stark warning about what happens when politics thinks it has graduated from accountability to God as the murderous regimes of Stalin, Hitler and Mao display. That century reminds us that while there are dangers if religion becomes politics there are even more dangers if politics becomes religion. In the twenty-first century we have seen some groups claiming religious legitimacy for less extensive but nevertheless murderous actions despite being disowned by the mainstream religious traditions. What these examples show us is that both politics and religion need to be secularized, something we see beginning in Israel's story. In contrast both politics and religion need to be secularised. Israel's monotheism told its politicians, the monarchy, priests, religious authorities and prophets, that they could not claim to be God for the people.[7] Indeed all were subject to the Torah, the vision of God for Israel, while in the New Testament the cross of Jesus indicates that God's way was neither the Peace of Rome nor the religious vision of the High Priest's party. The Bible therefore secularised politics and religion long before seventeenth-century Europe. Yet this biblical secularising does not imply the absence of God from public life. Instead, God is present in political and religious life, but not in a way always presented nor in ways we can possess. Consequently we must be reserved about claiming too much about God's activity.

Prayer places politics and religion in a bigger story

Prayer furthermore reminds us that we are part of God's story which positions and challenges us as political and religious leaders. Prayer reminds us that we are creatures in rather than creators of this story and so need to ask for God's help. Today, amnesia rather than atheism is the greater challenge for people of faith. We are exposed to so much change and choice that it is difficult to remember that we are part of God's bigger story. This is why we need to gather week by week in Church in order to be reminded of this story God, which has shaped our society.

POLITICS, POWER AND POVERTY[8]

Politics and power are about human beings and their social good, however contested the vision of that good life is. Christians believe that it matters to God that societies flourish in good ways. This is why Christians continue to be involved in politics and the exercise of power.

Politics is about ordering society for its good

Politics is the way we organize society. It is derived from the Greek word *polis* which means a city or an ordered form of community life. All societies need order to flourish and this can be seen throughout Scripture. For example Deuteronomy is a book shaped as a sort of treaty or covenant between God and his people modelled on ancient covenant treaties of the eighth century BC. It gave Israel a vision of an ordered social life which enabled them to live justly and rightly before God and with one another. Indeed Deuteronomy is a treatise on how to love God and love neighbour. Acts Chapter 28 on the other hand recognizes the importance of order in the Roman Empire. It relates the story of Paul safely travelling to Rome to put his case about his faith to the Emperor. This was only possible because of the Peace of Rome and because he was a citizen of Rome and therefore had recognized legal rights. Rome was an ordered empire which, for all its faults, actually represented a reasonable quality of life for most people compared to other options at the time. This is why writers like Luke portray Rome in a relatively good light, even though they also show Rome's failure to observe justice in the execution of Jesus.

IN PUBLIC

Power is accountable

Politics involves the exercise of power in pursuit of a just society. In the Rome of Paul's day, this Peace of Rome was embodied in law, military strength and a particular understanding of justice. The Emperor, the Senate and the whole administrative structure of the Roman Empire were designed to mediate power from the top to the bottom. Israel also had a deep sense of justice and right living expressed in their legal system called Torah. Deuteronomy literally means the 'second version of the Torah or law'. In both societies power was accountable to more than those who exercised it. This can be summarized as accountability to the One, the Many and the Few.[9]

The One was the source of sovereignty and the seat of all power. This was God for Israel or the gods for Rome (though this was confused when the emperor claimed to be a god). The Many in Rome were the citizens and in Israel the people of God charged to love their neighbours as themselves. The Few in both Rome and Israel were subgroups of society who embodied wisdom and were committed to excellence. For Rome these were senators, the army, the local governors and administrators such as Publius who is mentioned in Acts Chapter 28. For Israel these were the educators, the prophets, the priests and the military. These were what we would now call civil society. Such groups advised the executive, in Rome the emperor and in Israel the monarchy, in the art of good government.

Poverty tests the health of a society

Yet what distinguished Israel's politics and use of power from Rome's was a fourth group to whom those in power were accountable. These are called the poor or those in any society who have little if any power. In Deuteronomy they are described as the 'foreigner, the widow and the fatherless or orphaned'.[10] These groups were the most vulnerable in ancient society and Israel's politics were judged by God in terms of their impact upon them. This was God standing as guardian of the powerless to ensure that they could live in Israelite society with dignity. To underline this, Israel are reminded that they themselves were once powerless as slaves in Egypt and so must never forget these poor. For Christians politics and power must be further understood in the light of the life, death and resurrection of Jesus. This is a vision of politics as service for the good of all in society, not just some, and is judged by whether it makes possible a life of dignity for the poor. It is this vision of politics which has held English politics to account for centuries and is symbolised by an anointed monarchy. Such a view was absent from the Roman Empire and this was the reason according to Augustine of Hippo that it collapsed in the fourth century AD since Roman public service was not service for all people, but rather was service for an elite minority who used it to feather their nests often at the expense of the poor.

A CHRISTIAN VISION OF MONARCHY.[11]

'In my first Christmas Broadcast in 1952, I asked the people of the Commonwealth and Empire to pray for me as I prepared to dedicate myself to their service at my Coronation. I have been – and remain – very grateful to you for your prayers and to God for His steadfast love. I have indeed seen His faithfulness.' So wrote the late Queen in the Introduction to *The Servant Queen and the King she Serves* published in 2016 as a tribute for Her Majesty's 90th Birthday. It is as a servant of God and her people that the Queen sought to be remembered. The Queen was always a person sensitive to God's call on her life as monarch and throughout that life her faith has shaped her calling. Monarchy and service have a long pedigree in Jewish Christian thinking and service are stitched into our society's understanding of the role of the Monarch. Indeed when monarchs sit on the throne in the robing room in Parliament they face a picture of Christ on the Cross. This sets before them the challenge to be a Servant Monarch who is a sign of the Servant God Christians worship. As Monarchs they are the sign of sovereignty in service in our society.

A SIGN OF GOD'S SOVEREIGNTY: MONARCHY SIGNS THE SACRED IN OUR MIDST

Human monarchy was not welcomed by all in ancient Israel as we see in 1 Samuel 8–10. For some, human monarchy rivalled God's monarchy and challenged the idea that the Lord is King. This can be seen in Deuteronomy 17:14–20 which includes the dangers of abusive monarchy in its charter for a good Monarch. Yet for others in Israel's history the Monarch was the anointed one, the Messiah, the figure responsible for ensuring that the nation kept faith with God. And it is this latter tradition which we see in the anointing of our own Monarch at the coronation, since the Monarch is not simply accountable to the people but to God. Sadly our history is riddled with Monarchs whose focus was on themselves rather than on God and constitutional monarchy is an attempt to check such abuses by keeping the symbol of servant sovereignty separate from the exercise of political power.

A SIGN OF OUR SOCIETY AND ITS STORY

In many ancient societies the Monarch was a sort of corporate person in whom all were present. Monarchs represented all and in many communities owned society and its members. In the past in Uganda the local king of the Baganda, the

ON YOUR BIKE

Kabaka, used to regard his people as an extension of himself and therefore available for him to do whatever he wanted with them. In the late nineteenth century the Ugandan boy martyrs resisted this view by asserting that their bodies were no longer the property of the king but belonged to Christ. As a consequence the *Kabaka* ordered them to be dismembered and burnt alive at Namogongo outside Kampala, now a martyrs' memorial. The legacy of Christian influence in these islands is that the Monarch is now the people's servant rather than their owner. When people see or meet the Monarch they sense that they are in touch with a human being whose story carries our story as the people of these islands who acknowledge the sovereignty of God as revealed to us in the story of Israel and Jesus Christ.

ECONOMICS: BUILDING A HOME TOGETHER[12]

Building a home together is a challenge for any society and is properly the function of economics which, in Greek, means 'building a home together'.[13] For Christians this home must be built in a way faithful to the vision of God's kingdom which God Jesus Christ embodied.

A kneeling economics focused on God

All economic visions make claims about what the good, true and beautiful society or communal home looks like. Christians, following ancient Israel, assert that the Ten Commandments give us a vision of the good society which has stood the test of time and has shown itself capable of building the good society which is rooted in love for God and for neighbour. We see this in microcosm in Church Schools as they centre their life on the worship of God. Many of the pupil's parents are not churchgoers. However they value this kneeling economics which builds the sort of home they want their children to be part of.

A liberating economics focused on human flourishing

The Ten Commandments imagined a society in which all could flourish, including the outsider or stranger. Yet in the time of Jesus, as on many occasions before in Israel's story, this vision had been corrupted by interest groups with other agendas. In John Chapter 2 we read of the cleansing of the Temple when Jesus casts out those who exploited worshippers by charging extortionate rates to change ordinary currency into temple money to pay for sacrificial animals. Instead of encouraging human flourishing this was an economics which oppressed and exploited the vulnerable. As someone who lived in Uganda and in South Africa during traumatic periods of their history, I have seen the impact of bad economics on vulnerable people. And in our own part of the world we also need to be on our guard against this for example by championing the Living Wage campaign and supporting Credit Unions. Indeed as Philip Blond, a thinker on the right of politics argues, good economics is not about 'flying blind capitalism' but is about a 'conservatism for the poor'.[14] Consequently building a home together is tested by how this home liberates human flourishing.

A social economics focused on the common good

The Ten Commandments were first and foremost Israel's economic charter and the story of Israel is the story of how this particular society sought to build a home together which honoured their Lord. This home, though, was not simply to be for themselves, but as the 'light to lighten the Gentiles': their witness was to open the door to all people.[15] Yet they struggled to attract these Gentiles or make space for them and by the time of Jesus, the Temple, which was to draw all people to worship the one God, was simply a draw for the Jewish community with

Gentiles kept at bay in the outer courtyard. The story of Jesus is the story of how this limited economy was blown apart. 'Destroy this temple and in three days I will raise it up', this rebuilt temple being Jesus himself.[16] The New Testament is therefore the story of a community which discovered that in Jesus a home for all people is now possible, a social economics focused on the common good. This common good 'is not the right of individuals to own their goods but is the right of society to be social.'[17] It is to see ourselves as a community who share a common story rather than a collective of people who gather for transitory, transactional purposes

A CHRISTIAN VISION OF VOLUNTEERING[8]

Volunteering is important to society and to the Christian faith because volunteering goes to the heart of the sort of society or communal home we want to build together. As noted above, the word for building a home is economics since economics comes from two Greek words, *oikos* meaning a house or home and *nomos* meaning law or order. Economics therefore is about building a home together in which we can all flourish. So what sorts of economics make for good home building?

COMMERCE

Commerce is the economics of buying and selling using money to pay for things. Commerce happens in markets which distribute goods and services using price as a measure of value. This activity is what most people think economics is all about if you follow TV/Radio or internet, etc. Yet it is not enough on its own to make a good home since it values people by the size of their pockets and reduces people to competitive consumers.

IN PUBLIC

TAX

Taxation is the economics of the state which takes money from its citizens and redistributes it to ensure that services and resources are provided for all citizens. This helps to protect vulnerable people from the ups and downs of life and ties the rich and powerful into social responsibility. Yet it is not enough on its own to make a good home since it can lead to a sense of powerlessness as ordinary people feel marginal to decision making about tax rates and spends.

GIVING

Giving is the economics of civil society where individuals and groups freely give or volunteer their time, money and energy to enable people around them to have a better quality of life. Volunteering makes a major contribution to society, something which has become even more apparent during the COVID-19 pandemic. For example, according to the National Council for Volunteer Organisations (NCVO), the 2017-18 financial value of volunteering to our society was £18.2 billion which was more than the nominal Gross Domestic Product of Iceland.[19] Yet for most of us the money is not the issue. It is the gift freely offered of time, skills, energy, gifts, donations etc. Giving/volunteering build community in a way buying and selling or taxing and providing don't.

Consequently Christians have always seen charitable giving or free giving as vital for building a good home together. Commerce and taxation have moral value and purpose but on their own they cannot build a good society/a good home together since they are based on calculation and self-interest. Volunteering is about something deeper. It builds community and brings joy, blessing and thanksgiving to giver and receiver. And it is closest to the way Christians believe God relates to us seen most clearly in the gift of Jesus to the world. Yet giving on its own or alongside commerce and taxation is not enough since each can fool us into thinking that we know what good means and so can build a good home on our own.

PRAYER

So we need another form of economics, the economics of prayer. Prayer is key to how we build a home together with God since in prayer we learn what good looks like to God. Prayer enables us to see that the good life is to love God and to love our neighbours as ourselves. This is at the heart of the Lord's Prayer and is why Isaiah told the ancient people of God, Israel, to build a home together which honoured God. So it is very apt to celebrate volunteering in a church, a public place of prayer and a sign of the story of Jesus and his followers which has infused our civil society for centuries.

Economics therefore is about building a home together and volunteering is vital to this homebuilding since it builds community in a distinctive and enriching way. It reflects the giving of God which we are called to emulate. We certainly need commerce and taxation in our complex world to ensure goods and services are distributed and shared as efficiently and fairly as possible. Yet we also need a deeper and bigger economics, the economics of prayer, which shares this homebuilding with God who has given us everything, our lives, gifts, skills and world.

LUKE AND LEGAL[20]

'Justice is a key component of a society which is marked by the common good. Achieving justice ... involves reflective assessment on issues, within the context of a clear moral framework. In Western societies that framework is still largely derived from the Judaeo-Christian tradition'. So wrote Sir Philip Mawer in *On Rock or Sand: Firm Foundations for Britain's Future* edited by the former Archbishop of York.[21]

JUSTICE IS STITCHED INTO CREATION

The Jews' great gift to the world was to conceive of reality as essentially moral and accountable rather than arbitrary and chaotic. Justice and righteousness are central to everything because they are grounded in the very identity of the one God. Justice is not simply the expression of human will. Indeed monotheism, as former Chief Rabbi Jonathan Sacks asserts stops right equalling might and instead roots right in the divine who is not in the pocket of any human power.[22] This is Isaiah's vision of God in Isaiah Chapter 5, God who invites all who thirst to come to his waters, to his vision of reality expressed and remembered in the story of Israel's encounter with this God. This is the One the prophet challenges the people to seek and to get right with, a liturgical formula inviting worshippers to listen to the Torah or Law or God's just ordering of reality. And this Torah, as Psalm19 indicates, infuses creation and the good society. The two cohere rather than conflict.

The practice of justice therefore is key to a good society since justice underlines the moral character of created reality, its origin in God and the responsibilities this asks of us. As Rowan Williams asserts the task of the Criminal Justice System is to build responsibility which is social as well as personal and to register crime as those actions which break this relationship and subvert this fundamental responsibility.[23]

HUMAN JUSTICE IS PROVISIONAL NOT ABSOLUTE.

St Luke's prologue to the story of Jesus reveals that to be human is to be situated. We are always somewhere physically and in time rather than having an anywhere, universal view of reality and this is why we make sense of our lives through stories which locate us in time and place. Indeed Christians believe that we encounter God as Jesus in time and place and this is what we mean by incarnation. Yet these stories, particularly the core stories of faith in our Scriptures, show that we are not simply limited or finite. We are also fallen. As a result we only see truth in part rather than fully and our sight is never pure. Is this why the statue of Justice at the Old Bailey is blindfolded; as a sign of impartiality in the dispensing of justice and yet a reminder that all human justice is provisional, aspirational and imperfect?

This is also why Israel, whose name means 'the one who struggles' with God, argued with God about questions of justice, a struggle most remarkably seen in the story of Job and regularly expressed in the Psalms. Indeed Israel secularised political and legal powers by reminding them that their judgements were not the final word. Only God has the full and final judgement and human judgements gesture to this by their very contingent and contested character.

JESUS: GOD'S JUSTICE

For Christians the justice of God is most fully seen in the story of Jesus since he lived righteously as the true Israelite and his life was characterized by forgiveness as reconciliation. In so doing he fulfilled Israel's vocation to be a light to all people. Furthermore this story of Jesus as the true Israelite brought into being the Church, a community which actively seeks to follow and be shaped by that story. The gift of this community is to bear witness in its social life to Jesus' embodiment of the justice of God, a justice which seeks above all forgiveness and reconciliation, a justice which is beyond the law. This is the deepest response to wrongdoing because it re-establishes social healing and harmony which is the truest justice.

IN PUBLIC

Questions for reflection

1. How does your church discern and promote the common good in its area?
2. What do you think is the most important Christian insight about power and politics?
3. What would good economics look like in your local community?
4. How do the stories of Israel and Jesus help you understand the meaning of justice?

CHAPTER 10
In Conclusion

In this book I have used cycling as a lens through which to understand what it means to follow and serve Christ today. Following and serving Christ, like cycling, are about passion, flexibility, health, contemplation, practicality and character. Each develops as we are faced with new challenges and adventures in settings we are unfamiliar with. These test us and stretch us so that we grow more proficient and confident. They open up horizons which we were not aware of beforehand. They help us to appreciate the richness and specificity of people and places with their particular histories and stories. In so doing we find ourselves bound to these people and their places in a new way, a commitment which grasps us as much as it is chosen by us.

Following and serving Christ, like cycling, brings its own challenges, some of which cause us to suffer. Yet suffering is a reality check as it reminds us that we are not in a world of our own making or choosing. It also helps us to acknowledge our vulnerability and limitations and also the educational value of our struggles as we stay with them rather than denying or fleeing them. Suffering for Christians therefore opens up new insights into God as the one who is with us in our darkness as well as in the light, slowly forming us into self-giving, sacrificial people.

IN CONCLUSION

In this way our personal suffering enriches our faith and theological awareness, helping us to become more trusting and less self-preoccupied.

Following and serving Christ, like cycling is about companionship. We find ourselves to be part of a capacious community of fellow travellers helping each other gain confidence and make connections with others. For Christians this is about connecting the local with the global, the somewhere of the local church with the everywhere of the global church. Such connecting involves learning each other's languages so that we can communicate respectfully and better understand each other's situation, culture and heritage. Cycling and discipleship are embodied witnesses to forms of life which contrast with many of the assumptions and norms of contemporary society. This can make cyclists and disciples feel like resident aliens in their host societies. In consequence, cyclists and disciples recognise the importance of their core communities since the Church and the cycling community cultivate, nourish and sustain these distinct identities. Both also need leaders who guide their communities, keep alive the memory of their core stories, care for fellow travellers on the road and help their communities to be agents of change and embody wisdom and good character.

To follow and serve the incarnate Christ, like cycling, happens in the material world. The physicality of life in the Spirit means that Christian spirituality is honed through embracing the gifts of creation around us and mining them for insights into God. In particular silence, sound and sight provide opportunities for contemplation, prayer, praise, gratitude, lament, community and learning which enable us better to follow and serve Christ in our lives. We are thereby crafted by the Spirit into signs of the Gospel, which help others to see the material difference being a

ON YOUR BIKE

Christian makes as an evangelistic witness to the love of God for the world.

To be a follower and serve Christ today leads us into rough terrain. We can feel that we are on trial as we try to speak the truth as we see it and support our convictions with persuasive, evidenced-based arguments. Sadly, in an impatient, overconfident world, patient exploration of issues may not always get a hearing. However, Christians believe that naked assertion must not replace careful, reasoned, evidence-based argument since God stands guardian of the truth. This is also why Christians continue to engage with public issues in their societies since, like cyclists, they are part of public life. Both are committed to building a world in which the vulnerable and creation are respected, the common good means the good of all rather than some, power is exercised wisely, law is just and virtue is rewarded.

Cycling has so much to teach disciples and ministers of Christ. I hope that this book will encourage more Christians to get on their bikes and find connections between following and serving Christ and cycling, at a time when all of us who can need to get on our bikes.

Select Bibliography

Attenborough, David with Hughes, Jonnie, *A Life on Our Planet: My Witness Statement and a Vision for the Future* (London: Ebury Publishing, 2020).

Avis, Paul, *Ecumenical Theology and the Elusiveness of Doctrine* (London: SPCK, 1986).
- *Authority, Leadership, Conflict in the Church* (London: Mowbray, 1992).

Bell, Charlie, *Queer Holiness: The Gift of LGBTQI People to the Church* (London: DLT, 2022).

Biggar, Nigel, *Colonialism: A Moral Reckoning* (London: William Collins, 2023).

Brueggemann, Walter, *The Land: Place as Gift, Promise, Challenge in Biblical Faith* (Fortress Press, 2002).
- *Theology of the Old Testament: Testimony, Dispute, Advocacy* (Philadelphia: Fortress Press, 1997).

Beaumont, Mark, *The Man who Cycled the World* (London: Bantam Press, 2009).

Beeley, Christopher A., *Leading God's People: Wisdom*

for the Early Church for Today (Grand Rapids, MI: Eerdmans, 2012).

Cain, Susan, *The Power of Introverts in a World That Can't Stop Talking* (London: Penguin Books, 2012).

Campbell, Alastair V., *The Gospel of Anger* (London: SPCK, 1986).

Carney, Mark, *Value(s): Climate, Credit, Covid and How we Focus on what Matters* (London: William Collins, 2021).

Collins, Jim, *From Good to Great* (London: Random House Business Books, 2001).

Croft, Steven, *Together in Love and Faith: Personal Reflections and Next Steps for the Church* (Oxford: Bishop of Oxford, 2022).

Dante Alighieri, *The Divine Comedy* (Oxford: Oxford University Press, 1998 edn.).

Davie, Grace, *The Sociology of Religion* (London: Sage, 2007).

Davison, Andrew, *Amazing Love: Theology for Understanding Discipleship, Sexuality and Mission* (London: DLT, 2016).

Davison, Andrew, and Milbank, Alison, *For the Parish: A Critique of Fresh Expressions* (London: SCM, 2010).

Deenan, Patrick J., *Why Liberalism Failed* (Yale and London: Yale University Press, 2018).

SELECT BIBLIOGRAPHY

Daniels, Robin, *The Virgin Eye: Towards a Contemplative View of Life* (Watford: Instant Apostle, 2016).

Dormor, Duncan and Morris, Jeremy, *An Acceptable Sacrifice? Homosexuality and the Church* (London: SPCK, 2007).

Edwards, James R., *From Christ to Christianity: How the Jesus Movement Became the Church in Less than a Century* (Grand Rapids MI: Baker Academic, 2021).

Gallagher, Michael P., *Dive Deeper: The Human Poetry of Faith* (London: DLT, 2001).

Goddard, Andrew, *Homosexuality and the Church of England* (Cambridge: Grove Booklets, 2004).

Gill, Robin, *Churchgoing and Christian Ethics* (Cambridge: Cambridge University Press, 1999).

Goodhart, David, *The Road to Somewhere: The Populist Revolt and the Future of Politics* (London: C Hirst & Co (Publishers Ltd, 2017).
- *Head, Hand, Heart: The Struggle for Dignity in the 21st Century* (London: Allen Lane, 2020).

Gray, John, *Enlightenment's Wake: Politics and Culture at the Close of the Modern Age* (Abingdon: Routledge, 1995).
- *Seven Types of Atheism* (London: Penguin, 2019).

Grundy, Malcolm, *Understanding Congregations: A New Shape for the Local Church* (London: Mowbray, 1998).
- *What's New in Church Leadership: Creative*

ON YOUR BIKE

Responses to the Changing Pattern of Church Life (Norwich: Canterbury Press, 2007).
- *Leadership and Oversight: New Models for Episcopal Ministry* (London: Mowbray, 2011).

Hardy, Daniel W., *Finding the Church,* (London: SCM, 2001).
- 'A Magnificent Complexity: Letting God be God in Church, Society and Creation' in Ford. David F. and Stamps, Dennis L. (eds.), *Essentials of Christian Community. Essays for Daniel Hardy* (Edinburgh: T & T Clark, 1996).

Hardy, Daniel W., and Ford, David F., *Jubilate, Theology in Praise* (London: Darton, Longman and Todd, 1984).

Hardy, Daniel W., with Ford, Deborah Hardy, Ochs, Peter and Ford, David, *Wording a Radiance: Parting Conversations on God and the Church* (London: SCM, 2010).

Hauerwas, Stanley, *Vision and Virtue: Essays in Christian Ethical Reflection* (Notre Dame: University of Notre Dame Press, 1981).
- *A Community of Character, Toward a Constructive Christian Social Ethic*, 4th edn. (Notre Dame: University of Notre Dame Press, 1986).
- *Suffering Presence: Theological Reflections on Medicine, the Mentally Handicapped and the Church* (Edinburgh: T & T Clark, 1988).
- *Naming the Silences: God, Medicine and the Problem of Suffering*, 2nd edn. (Edinburgh: T&T Clark, 1993).

Heaney, Robert S. and William L. Sachs, *The Promise of Anglicanism* (London: SCM, 2019).

SELECT BIBLIOGRAPHY

Hunter, James D., *To Change the World: The Irony, Tragedy and Possibility of Christianity in the Late Modern World* (Oxford: OUP, 2010).

Hytner, Richard, *Consiglieri: Leading from the Shadows* (London: Profile Books, 2014).

Impey, Richard, *How to Develop Your Local Church: Working with the Wisdom of the Congregation* (London: SPCK, 2010).

Inge, John, *A Christian Theology of Place* (Aldershot: Ashgate, 2003).

Jones, James, *Jesus and the Earth* (London: SPCK, 2003).

Kaiser, Kevin and S. David Young, *The Blue Line Imperative: What Managing for Value Really Means* (Chichester: Wiley & Sons, 2016).

Keating, Thomas, *Open Mind: Open Heart* (London: Bloomsbury, 2006).

Long, D. Stephen, *The Art of Cycling, Living and Dying: Moral Theology from Everyday Life* (Eugene, Oregon: Cascade Books, 2021).

Lowney, Chris, *Pope Francis: Why He Leads the Way He Leads* (Chicago: Loyola Press, 2013).

MacCulloch, Diarmaid, *Silence: A Christian History* (London: Penguin, 2014).

Makhuba, Paul, *Who are the Independent Churches?* (Johannesburg: Skotaville, 1988).

Matthew, Iain, *The Impact of God: Soundings from St John of the Cross* (London: Hodder & Stoughton Ltd, 2010).

Mayne, Michael, *A Year Lost and Found* (London: Darton, Longman and Todd, 2007).

McGrath, Alister E., *The Blackwell Encyclopedia of Modern Christian Thought* (Oxford: Blackwell Publishers, 1993).

McIntosh, Mark A., *Discernment and Truth: The Spirituality and Theology of Knowledge* (Publish Drive, 2004).

Milbank, John, *Theology and Social Theory: Beyond Secular Reason* (Oxford: Blackwell, 1990).

Milbank, John and Pabst, Adrian, *The Politics of Virtue: Post Liberalism and the Human Face* (London: Rowman & Littlefield, 2016).

Moisés, Naím, *The End of Power* (New York: Basic Books, 2013).

Moore, Gareth, *A Question of Truth: Christianity and Homosexuality* (London: Continuum, 2003).

Morisy, Anne, *Bewildered and Troubled: Enacting Hope in Troubled Times* (London: Continuum, 2009).

Moberley, R.W.L., *The Gift of the Old Testament: Encountering the Divine in Christian Scripture* (MI: Baker Academic, 2020).

SELECT BIBLIOGRAPHY

Moynagh, Michael, with Harrold, Philip, *A Church for Every Context: An Introduction to Theology and Practice* (London: SCM, 2012).

Murray, Douglas, *The Strange Death of Europe: Immigration, Identity, Islam* (London: Bloomsbury Continuum, 2018).

O'Donovan, Oliver, *Resurrection and the Moral Order: An Outline for Evangelical Ethics,* 2nd edn (Leicester: Apollos, 1994).
- *The Desire of Nations: Rediscovering the Roots of Political Theology* (Cambridge: Cambridge University Press, 1996).
- *The Ways of Judgment* (Cambridge: Eerdmans, 2005).

Pedrick, Claire and Blanch, Su, *How to Make Great Appointments in the Church: Calling, Competence and Chemistry* (London: SPCK, 2011).

Percy, Martyn, *Shaping the Church: The Promise of Implicit Theology* (Farnham: Ashgate, 2010).

Radner, Ephraim, *Hope Among the Fragments: The Broken Church and its Engagement of Scripture* (Grand Rapids, MI: Brazos Press, 2004).

Radner, Ephraim and Turner, Philip, *The Fate of Communion: The Agony of Anglicanism and the Future of a Global Church* (Cambridge: Eerdmans, 2006).

Rohr, Richard, *Falling Upwards: A Spirituality for the Two Halves of Life* (London; SPCK, 2012).

Rooms, Nigel, *The Faith of the English: Integrating Christ and Culture* (London: SPCK, 2011).

Ross, Maggie, *Silence: A User's Guide* (London: Darton, Longman and Todd, 2014).

Sacks, Jonathan, *Not in God's Name: Confronting Religious Violence* (London: Hodder & Stoughton Ltd, 2015).
- *Morality: Restoring the Common Good in Divided Times* (London: Hodder & Stoughton Ltd, 2020).

The Power of Ideas: Words of Faith and Wisdom (London: Hodder and Stoughton, 2022).

Sadgrove, Michael, *Wisdom and Ministry: The Call to Leadership* (London: SPCK, 2008).

Sandel, Michael J., *The Tyranny of Merit: What's Become of the Common Good* (London: Allen Lane, 2020).

Sanneh, Lamin, *Translating the Message: The Missionary Impact on Culture* (Maryknoll, New York: Orbis Books, 1990).

Sentamu, John, ed., *On Rock or Sand? Firm Foundations for Britain's Future* (2015).

Siedentop, Larry, *Inventing the Individual: The Origins of Western Liberalism* (London: Penguin, 2015).

St John of the Cross, *Dark Night of the Soul*, 3rd edn. (Tunbridge Wells: Burns & Oates, 1985).

SELECT BIBLIOGRAPHY

Scruton, Roger, *Where We Are: The State of Britain Now* (London: Bloomsbury, 2017).

Sheldrake, Philip, *Spaces for the Sacred: Place, Memory and Identity* (Baltimore, Maryland: The John Hopkins University Press, 2001).

Standing, Guy, *The Precariat: The New Dangerous Class* (London: Bloomsbury Academic, 2011).

Taylor, John V., *The Go Between God* (London: SCM, 1972).
The Christlike God (London: SCM, 2004).

Taylor, Charles, *A Secular Age* (London: Belknap Press, 2007).

Thatcher, Adrian, *God, Sex and Gender: An Introduction* (Chichester: Wiley-Blackwell, 2011).
Thiselton, Anthony C., *The Hermeneutics of Doctrine* (Cambridge, Eerdmans, 2007).

Thomson, John B., *The Ecclesiology of Stanley Hauerwas: A Christian Theology of Liberation* (Aldershot: Ashgate, 2003).
- *Church on Edge? Practising Ministry Today* (London: Darton, Longman and Todd, 2004).
- *DOXA: A Discipleship Course* (London: Darton, Longman and Todd, 2007).
Living Holiness: Stanley Hauerwas and the Church (London: Epworth, 2010).
- *Sharing Friendship: Exploring Anglican Character, Vocation, Witness and Mission* (Farnham: Ashgate, 2015).
- 'Friendship in Fragility: A Gospel for the North?' in Wakefield, Gavin and Rooms, eds., *Northern Gospel:*

Northern Church (Durham: Sacristy Press, 2016), pp. 93--95.

Tomlin, Graham and Backhouse, Stephen, *Why the Church Should Care About Housing* (Cambridge: Grove Booklets, 2021).

Valerio, Ruth, *Saying Yes to Life* (London: SPCK, 2020).
Vanstone, William H., *The Stature of Waiting* (London: Darton, Longman and Todd, 2004).

Vasey, Michael, *Strangers and Friends: A New Exploration of Homosexuality and the Bible* (London: Hodder and Stoughton, 1995).

Walker, Peter and Goddard, Andrew, *True Union in the Body? A Contribution to the discussion within the Anglican Communion concerning the public blessing of same-sex relationships* (Cambridge: Grove Booklets, 2003).

Walton, Roger, *Discipleship Together: Discipleship, Formation and Small Groups* (London: SPCK, 2014).

Ward, Pete, *God's Behaving Badly: Media, Religion and Celebrity Culture* (London: SCM, 2011).

Wells, Samuel, *Improvisation: The Drama of Christian Ethics* (London: SPCK, 2004).
- *Incarnational Ministry: Being with the Church* (Norwich: Canterbury Press, 2017).

Weil, Simone, *The Need for Roots* (London & New York: Routledge, 2002).

SELECT BIBLIOGRAPHY

Williams, Rowan, *Arius: Heresy and Tradition* (London: DLT, 1987).

- *Silence and Honey Cakes: The Wisdom of the Desert* (Oxford: Lion, 2003).
- *Faith in the Public Square* (London: Bloomsbury, 2012).
The Edge of Words: God and the Habits of Language (London: Bloomsbury, 2014).
- *Meeting God in Paul* (London: SPCK, 2015).
- *Being Disciples*, (London: SPCK, 2016).
- *On Augustine* (London: Bloomsbury, 2016).
- *Holy Living: The Christian Tradition for Today* (London: Bloomsbury, 2017).
- *Christ the Heart of Creation* (London: Bloomsbury, 2018).

Williams, Rowan, and Elliot, Larry, eds., *Crisis and Recovery: Ethics, Economics and Justice* (Basingstoke: Palgrave MacMillan, 2010).

Willimon, William, *Pastor: The Theology and Practice of Ordained Ministry* (Nashville, TN: Abingdon Press, 2002).

Winkett, Lucy, *Our Sound is Our Wound: Contemplative Listening to a Noisy World* (London: Continuum, 2010).

Zuboff, Shoshana, *The Age of Surveillance Capitalism: The Fight for a Human Future at the New Frontier of Power* (London: Profile Books Ltd, 2019).

Notes

PREFACE
John B. Thomson, *The Ecclesiology of Stanley Hauerwas: A Christian Theology of Liberation* (Aldershot: Ashgate, 2003); *Church on Edge? Practising Ministry Today* (London: DLT, 2004); *DOXA: A Discipleship Course* (London: DLT, 2007); *Living Holiness: Stanley Hauerwas and the Church* (London: Epworth, 2010) and *Sharing Friendship: Exploring Anglican Character, Vocation, Witness and Mission* (Farnham: Ashgate, 2015).

CHAPTER 1: IN THE SADDLE
[1] Now called Cycling UK.
[2] These theological approaches argued that Christ sided with the poor and the oppressed, which in South Africa, was the majority black community. They also challenged the oppressors, which, in South Africa, was the minority white community. Commonly called Liberation Theologies, those I particularly encountered in this regard were Black Theology and African Theology, though much Feminist Theology also used similar arguments about gender. For a brief survey of South African Theologies of this time see John B. Thomson, 'Protestant Theology: South Africa' in Alister E. McGrath, *The Blackwell Encyclopedia of Modern Christian Thought* (Oxford: Blackwell Publishers, 1993), pp. 520–24.
[3] I owe these insights to Graham Pigott.

CHAPTER 2: IN FORMATION

[1] Graham Tomlin and Stephen Backhouse, *Why the Church Should Care About Housing*, (Cambridge: Grove Booklets, 2021), p.15.

[2] Matthew 5:43–8.

[3] The town was officially renamed Makhanda in memory of Xhosa warrior and prophet Makhanda ka Nxele.

[4] Ciskei along with the Transkei among others were called Bantustans, or areas for black Africans, and were the way the apartheid regime argued that each race was able to govern its own people. They were never viable economically with poor land and infrastructure and so were always dependent on white South Africa.

[5] Robert S. Heaney and William L. Sachs, *The Promise of Anglicanism* (London: SCM, 2019), p. 221.

[6] Lamin Sanneh, *Translating the Message: The Missionary Impact on Culture* (Maryknoll, New York: Orbis Books, 1990). For a critical and contentious discussion of Colonialism see Nigel Biggar, *Colonialism: A Moral Reckoning* (London: William Collins, 2023) who likewise contests the view that missionaries were simply uncritical agents of imperialism offering a more nuanced view which acknowledges their culturally situatedness yet also notes that their commitment to living with and learning the languages and cultures of local people often led to clashes with colonial authorities about policy.

[7] J.V. Taylor, *The Go Between God* (London: SCM, 1972).

CHAPTER 3: IN MINISTRY

[1] See David Goodhart, *The Road to Somewhere: The Populist Revolt and the Future of Politics* (London: C Hirst & Co (Publishers Ltd, 2017) for a discussion on the difference between Anywhere and Somewhere people.

[2] See John Inge, *A Christian Theology of Place* (Aldershot: Ashgate, 2003) and Philip Sheldrake, *Spaces for the*

NOTES

    Sacred: Place, Memory and Identity (Baltimore, Maryland: The John Hopkins University Press, 2001).

[3] See John B. Thomson, 'Friendship in Fragility: A Gospel for the North?' in Gavin Wakefield and Nigel Rooms, eds., *Northern Gospel: Northern Church* (Durham: Sacristy Press, 2016), pp. 93–95.

[4] *From Anecdote to Evidence: finds from the Church Growth Research Programme, 2011-2013*, http://www.churchgrowthresearch.org.uk/UserFiles/File/Reports/FromAnecdoteToEvidence1.0.pdf, p. 10. The 'solutions' to the challenges this report presents have merit but need to be tempered by local realities particularly in rural areas.

[5] Guy Standing, *The Precariat: The New Dangerous Class* (London: Bloomsbury Academic, 2011).

[6] Standing (2011), pp. 132–47.

[7] See Matt. 28:20.

[8] James Davison Hunter, *To Change the World: The Irony, Tragedy and Possibility of Christianity in the Late Modern World* (Oxford: OUP, 2010), pp. 273–86. See also Thomson (2007) which uses the liturgy for formative catechesis.

[9] Charles Taylor, *A Secular Age* (London: Belknap Press, 2007), pp. 25–51, 62–89.

[10] Martyn Percy, *Shaping the Church: The Promise of Implicit Theology* (Farnham: Ashgate, 2010), pp. 39, 56.

[11] See Inge (2003), pp. 101–14.

[12] https://www.tearfund.org/en/media/press_releases/many_brits_look_to_faith_during_lockdown/

[13] Michael Moynagh with Philip Harrold, *A Church for Every Context: An Introduction to Theology and Practice* (London: SCM, 2012), p. 91.

[14] See Samuel Wells, *Incarnational Ministry: Being with the Church* (Norwich: Canterbury Press, 2017).

[15] See Thomson (2004), pp. 65–67 and (2010), pp. 88–91.

[16] See Thomson (2003).

[17] The word translated as 'have this mind' in the Christ Hymn

of Philippians 1:5–11 is the Greek word '*phronesis*' which is best understood as practical wisdom or learning through walking a particular journey.

[18] I am grateful to Revd Graham Pigott for helping me to distil these four themes.

[19] Thomson (2007).

[20] *Faith in the Countryside: Report of the Archbishop's Commission on Rural Areas* (Worthing: Churchman Publishing, 1990), p. 243.

[21] www.gov.uk/government/statistics/agriculture-in-the-united-kingdom-2021/chapter-3-farming-income#summary

[22] For the statistics in this article see: www.gov.uk/government/statistics/rural-poverty and https://assets.publishing.service.gov.uk/government/uploads/system/uploads/attachment_data/file/684003/future-farming-environment-consult-document.pdf

[23] https://www.tearfund.org/en/media/press_releases/many_brits_look_to_faith_during_lockdown/

[24] Paul Avis, *Ecumenical Theology and the Elusiveness of Doctrine* (London: SPCK, 1986), p. 43.

[25] This is at the heart of 'Engaging with the Past to Shape the Future: The Experience of Building on History: The Church in London' project which seeks to root contemporary debates about mission and ministry in the context of history so that new ways forward can take place in a grounded and reflective way. For further details see www.open.ac.uk/buildingonhistory

[26] See Inge (2003) and Sheldrake (2001).

[27] See https://www.christiantoday.com/article/linda-woodhead-the-church-of-england-is-on-its-last-chance/41437.htm

[28] For an exploration of the themes of context and contest within Anglicanism see Heaney and Sachs (2019).

NOTES

CHAPTER 4: IN SUFFERING

[1] For a moving memoir and reflection on cycling and Moral Theology following a severe health impact, see D. Stephen Long, *The Art of Cycling, Living and Dying: Moral Theology from Everyday Life* (Eugene Oregon: Cascade Books, 2021).

[2] Dante Alighieri, *The Divine Comedy* (Oxford: Oxford University Press, 1998), pp. 194–5.

[3] See Michael Paul Gallagher, *Dive Deeper: The Human Poetry of Faith* (London: DLT, 2001).

[4] Thomas Keating, *Open Mind: Open Heart* (London: Bloomsbury, 2006) p. 72.

[5] S. of S.2:6.

[6] Rowan Williams, Introduction to John A.T. Robinson, *Thou Who Art: The Concept of the Personality of God* (London: Continuum, 2006), p. x.

[7] For a reflection on suffering see Stanley M. Hauerwas, *Suffering Presence: Theological Reflections on Medicine, the Mentally Handicapped and the Church* (Edinburgh: T & T Clark, 1988) and *Naming the Silences: God, Medicine and the Problem of Suffering*, 2nd edn (Edinburgh: T&T Clark, 1993).

[8] Gen. 32:26–32.

[9] Richard Rohr, *Falling Upwards: A Spirituality for the Two Halves of Life* (London; SPCK, 2012).

[10] St John of the Cross, *Dark Night of the Soul*, 3rd edn. (Tunbridge Wells, Burns & Oates, 1985). See also Iain Matthew, *The Impact of God: Soundings from St John of the Cross* (London: Hodder & Stoughton Ltd, 2010), pp. 51–58.

[11] Sam Wells, *Incarnational Ministry: Being with the Church* (Norwich: Canterbury Press, 2017), pp. 8–20.

[12] Michael Mayne, *A Year Lost and Found* (London: DLT, 2007), p.1

[13] Mayne (2007), pp. 12, 15.

[14] Mayne (2007), p. 44. See also W.H. Vanstone, *The Stature of Waiting* (London: DLT, 2004).
[15] Rowan Williams, *Christ the Heart of Creation* (London: Bloomsbury, 2018).
[16] Williams (2018), p. xiii.
[17] Williams (2018), pp. 226–228.
[18] Rowan Williams, *Holy Living: The Christian Tradition for Today* (London: Bloomsbury, 2017), p. 27.
[19] John V. Taylor, *The Christlike God* (London: SCM, 2004), p. 188.
[20] Taylor (2004), p. 193.
[21] Taylor (2004), pp. 193–204.
[22] John 21:15.
[23] Jonathan Sacks, *Morality: Restoring the Common Good in Divided Times* (London: Hodder & Stoughton Ltd, 2020) p. 255.
[24] Sacks (2020), p. 260.
[25] David Goodhart, *Head, Hand, Heart: The Struggle for Dignity and Status in the 21st Century* (London: Allen Lane, 2020). Ironically given the advances in Artificial Intelligence (AI) and the increasingly aging population, Hand and Heart roles may well become more significant than many Head roles going forward as the latter are replaced by AI and soft skills, which AI can't replicate, become more important.
[26] R.W.L Moberley, *The Gift of the Old Testament: Encountering the Divine in Christian Scripture* (MI: Baker Academic, 2020), pp. 125—164.
[27] I am indebted to Graham Pigott for these insights.

CHAPTER 5: IN COMPANY
[1] https://www.cyclinguk.org/history
[2] For an account of this see Thomson (2004).
[3] David Goodhart (2017).
[4] Roger Scruton, *Where We Are: The State of Britain Now* (London: Bloomsbury, 2017).

NOTES

[5] Douglas Murray, *The Strange Death of Europe: Immigration, Identity, Islam* (London: Bloomsbury Continuum, 2018).

[6] Goodhart (2017), p. 232.

[7] Simone Weil, *The Need for Roots* (London & New York, Routledge, 2002).

[8] Nigel Rooms, *The Faith of the English: Integrating Christ and Culture* (London: SPCK, 2011).

[9] I am grateful to Philip Lewis for this description.

[10] See especially Grace Davie, *The Sociology of Religion* (London: Sage, 2007), Robin Gill, *Churchgoing and Christian Ethics* (Cambridge: Cambridge University Press, 1999), David Martin, *The Future of Christianity: Reflections of Violence and Democracy, Religion and Secularisation* (Farnham: Ashgate, 2011), Martin Percy, *The Ecclesial Canopy: Faith, Hope, Charity* (Farnham: Ashgate, 2012) and Rooms (2011).

[11] To explore these themes further see John Milbank, *Theology and Social Theory: Beyond Secular Reason* (Oxford: Blackwell, 1990), *The Word Made Strange: Theology, Language, Culture* (Oxford: Blackwell, 1997), *Being Reconciled: Ontology and Pardon* (London: Routledge, 2003) and *The Future of Love: Essays in Political Theology* (London: SCM, 2009; Oliver O'Donovan, *Resurrection and the Moral Order: An Outline for Evangelical Ethics,* 2nd edn (Leicester: Apollos, 1994), *The Desire of Nations: Rediscovering the Roots of Political Theology* (Cambridge: Cambridge University Press, 1996) and *The Ways of Judgment* (Cambridge UK, Eerdmans, 2005); Rowan Williams, *Faith in the Public Square* (London: Bloomsbury, 2012) and *On Augustine* (London: Bloomsbury, 2016) and Larry Siedentop, *Inventing the Individual: The Origins of Western Liberalism* (London: Penguin, 2015).

[12] See Sanneh (1990).

[13] See Jonathan Sacks, *Not in God's Name: Confronting Religious Violence* (London: Hodder & Stoughton Ltd, 2015).

ON YOUR BIKE

14. Brad J. Kallenberg, *Ethics as Grammar: Changing the Postmodern Subject* (Notre Dame IND: University of Notre Dame Press, 2001), p. 156.
15. For a similar thesis see Patrick J. Deenan, *Why Liberalism Failed* (Yale and London: Yale University Press, 2018), pp. xiii, 5–13.
16. See the Final Report of the GRA:CE Project, *Growing Good: Growth, Social Action and Discipleship* (London: Theos, 2020) which argues that social action is evangelistic as it shows the story in action in a persuasive way to those beyond the church.
17. Thomson (2015).
18. See especially Anthony C. Thiselton, *The Hermeneutics of Doctrine* (Cambridge UK, Eerdmans, 2007), Grundy, Malcolm, *Understanding Congregations: A New Shape for the Local Church* (London: Mowbray, 1998), Richard Impey, *How to Develop Your Local Church: Working with the Wisdom of the Congregation* (London: SPCK, 2010) and Samuel Wells, *Improvisation: The Drama of Christian Ethics* (London: SPCK, 2004).
19. See David Goodhart, *Head, Hand, Heart: The Struggle for Dignity in the 21st Century* (London: Allen Lane, 2020).
20. See Williams (2012).
21. See also Jonathan Sacks (2020).
22. See Stanley Hauerwas, *A Community of Character, Toward a Constructive Christian Social Ethic*, 4th edn. (Notre Dame: University of Notre Dame Press, 1986) pp. 37.
23. For a rich account of Augustine's thinking see Williams (2016).
24. Williams (2012), p. 319 and (2018).
25. Williams (2017), p. 27.

CHAPTER 6: IN THE LEAD

1. Jonathan Sacks, *The Power of Ideas: Words of Faith and Wisdom* (London: Hodder and Stoughton, 2022), p. 86.
2. Mark 10:45.
3. Susan Cain, *The Power of Introverts in a World That Can't*

NOTES

    Stop Talking (London: Penguin Books, 2012).
4 Paul Avis, *Authority, Leadership, Conflict in the Church* (London: Mowbray, 1992), p. 131.
5 Mark Carney, *Value(s): Climate, Credit, Covid and How we Focus on what Matters* (London: William Collins, 2021), pp. 304–307.
6 Gregory the Great, *On Pastoral Care* 1 v2. Originally Titled *The Book of Pastoral Rule* translated by James Barmby. *From Nicene and Post-Nicene Fathers*, Second Series, Vol. 12. Edited by Philip Schaff and Henry Wace. (Buffalo, NY: Christian Literature Publishing Co., 1895).
7 Carney (2021), pp. 310-12.
8 Carney (2021), pp. 304-5.
9 See Claire Pedrick and Su Blanch, *How to Make Great Appointments in the Church: Calling, Competence and Chemistry* (London: SPCK, 2011).
10 Richard Hytner, *Consiglieri: Leading from the Shadows* (London: Profile Books, 2014).
11 Naím, Moisés, *The End of Power* (New York: Basic Books, 2013).
12 I am grateful to L. Gregory Jones for insights into wicked, hard and simple problems and to Mark de Rond of Cambridge University, for insights into what makes creative teams.
13 See Jim Collins, *From Good to Great* (London: Random House Business Books, 2001). For a reflection on leadership and wisdom in the Bible see Michael Sadgrove *Wisdom and Ministry: The Call to Leadership* (London: SPCK, 2008).
14 Samuel Wells (2017).
15 See Kevin Kaiser, and S. David Young, *The Blue Line Imperative: What Managing for Value Really Means* (Chichester: Wiley & Sons, 2016), pp. 208–18.
16 Malcolm Grundy, *What's New in Church Leadership: Creative Responses to the Changing Pattern of Church Life* (Norwich: Canterbury Press, 2007).
17 Christopher A. Beeley, *Leading God's People: Wisdom for*

the Early Church for Today (Grand Rapids, MI: Eerdmans, 2012), pp. vii–x. See also William Willimon, *Pastor: The Theology and Practice of Ordained Ministry* (Nashville, TN: Abingdon Press, 2002).

[18] Beeley (2012), p. 9.

[19] Beeley, (2012), pp. 59–78.

[20] See Chris Lowney, *Pope Francis: Why He Leads the Way He Leads* (Chicago: Loyola Press, 2013), p. 53 & p. 68 for Gerald Manley Hopkins quotation.

CHAPTER 7: IN THE SPIRIT

[1] For a rich reflection on silence and contemplation see Maggie Ross, *Silence: A User's Guide*, vol 1., (London: DLT, 2014).

[2] Rowan Williams, *The Edge of Words: God and the Habits of Language* (London: Bloomsbury, 2014).

[3] Ross (2014), p.26.

[4] I am grateful to Graham Pigott for these insights.

[5] Diarmaid MacCulloch, *Silence: A Christian History* (London: Penguin, 2014).

[6] The following are the verses quoted in order: Ps. 30:9, 1 Kings 18:26, Ps. 22:1–2, Isa. 53:7.

[7] Exod. 3:14.

[8] Mark 16:8.

[9] Mark 1:12–13.

[10] Matt. 5:48.

[11] 'Lord Jesus, Son of God have mercy on me a sinner.'

[12] Rowan Williams, *Silence and Honey Cakes: The Wisdom of the Desert* (Oxford: Lion, 2003).

[13] Isaac of Nineveh, Homily 64.

[14] Lucy Winkett, *Our Sound is Our Wound: Contemplative Listening to a Noisy World* (London: Continuum, 2010).

[15] Daniel W. Hardy, and Ford, David F., *Jubilate, Theology in Praise* (London: Darton, Longman &Todd, 1984), p. 1.

[16] John 1:1.

NOTES

[17] Winkett (2010), p. 15.
[18] Gen. 4: 1 and Jeremiah 31:15.
[19] Judg. 11:30–40.
[20] Rev 7:11–12.
[21] Winkett (2010), p. 119.
[22] Hardy & Ford (1984), p. 71.
[23] Hardy & Ford (1984), p. 19.
[24] Daniel W. Hardy, and Ford, David F., *Jubilate, Theology in Praise* (London: Darton, Longman &Todd, 1984) p. 107.
[25] See essays in P. Conradi, ed., *Existentialists and Mystics: Writings on Philosophy and Literature: Iris Murdoch* (London: Chatto & Windus, 1997).
[26] Stanley Hauerwas, *Vision and Virtue: Essays in Christian Ethical Reflection* (Notre Dame: University of Notre Dame Press, 1981).
[27] Gen.1:3.
[28] Exod. 3:1–2.
[29] Daniel W. Hardy with Deborah Hardy Ford, Peter Ochs and David Ford, *Wording a Radiance: Parting Conversations on God and the Church* (London: SCM, 2010), p. 49.
[30] I am grateful to Gordon Mursell for sharing these insights on the Fourth Gospel during a retreat he led.
[31] John 1:1–18.
[32] John 13:30.
[33] John 8:12; 9:5; 12:31–33.
[34] John 13:31; 17:1.
[35] John 3:2; 19:39.
[36] John 21:24.
[37] John 1:6, 29, 36.
[38] Rowan Williams, *Being Disciples*, (London: SPCK, 2016), p. 2.
[39] John 1:39.
[40] John 1:46.
[41] John 1:51; Gen. 28:12; John 12:20; John 20:6–8.
[42] John 12:35–36, 46.

[43] John 16:13; 20:29.
[44] Luke 24:30–31.
[45] Roger Walton, *Discipleship Together: Discipleship, Formation and Small Groups* (London: SPCK, 2014).
[46] Mark 1:17.
[47] Luke 24:53.
[48] John 13:34.
[49] Matthew 13:52.
[50] Mark A. McIntosh, *Discernment and Truth: The Spirituality and Theology of Knowledge* (2004).
[51] Daniel W. Hardy, 'A Magnificent Complexity: Letting God be God in Church, Society and Creation' in David F Ford and Stamps Dennis L., eds, *Essentials of Christian Community. Essays for Daniel Hardy* (Edinburgh: T & T Clark, 1996), pp. 307–56.
[52] Ford (1999), pp. 17–23.
[53] Pete Ward, *God's Behaving Badly: Media, Religion and Celebrity Culture* (London: SCM, 2011), p. 73.
[54] Robin Daniels, *The Virgin Eye: Towards a Contemplative View of Life* (Watford: Instant Apostle, 2016), p. 116.
[55] Goodhart (2017).
[56] Z. Bauman quoted in Anne Morisy, *Bewildered and Troubled: Enacting Hope in Troubled Times* (London: Continuum, 2009), pp. 9–10.
[57] Lev. 20:26.
[58] Walter Brueggemann, *The Land: Place as Gift, Promise, Challenge in Biblical Faith* (Fortress Press, 2002).
[59] Isa. 42:6; 49:6 and Gen.1.
[60] Hos. 6:6.
[61] Col 1:15–21.
[62] John 1:38; 12:27–36.
[63] Phil. 2:5–11.
[64] John 6:53.
[65] Acts 2:5–13, Gal. 3:28 and Rom. 14:3; 15:7.
[66] For an account of the remarkable way the Jesus sect became a global movement within a century see James

NOTES

R. Edwards, *From Christ to Christianity: How the Jesus Movement Became the Church in Less than a Century* (Grand Rapids MI: Baker Academic, 2021).
[67] Gal. 3:23.
[68] Rowan Williams, *Meeting God in Paul* (London: SPCK, 2015), p. 30.
[69] Rowan Williams, *Arius: Heresy and Tradition* (London: DLT, 1987), p. 239.
[70] Williams (2016), p. 54.
[71] Williams, (2003), p. 91.
[72] Inge (2003).
[73] Andrew Davison and Alison Milbank, *For the Parish: A Critique of Fresh Expressions* (London: SCM, 2010).
[74] Kallenberg (2001), p. 153.
[75] Williams (2016), p. 3.
[76] Williams (2016), pp. 12, 45.
[77] Daniel W. Hardy, *Finding the Church* (London: SCM, 2001), p. 19.
[78] Hardy (2001), p. 2.

CHAPTER 8: IN THE ROUGH

[1] Mark Beaumont, *The Man who Cycled the World* (London: Bantam Press, 2009).
[2] Shoshana Zuboff, *The Age of Surveillance Capitalism; The Fight for a Human Future at the New Frontier of Power* (London: Profile Books Ltd, 2019).
[3] Sacks (2020), pp.163--6.
[4] See Goodhart (2017).
[5] Sacks (2020), p.167.
[6] See A.C. Thiselton, 'Truth' in C. Brown, ed., *The New International Dictionary of New Testament Theology*, vol 3 (Exeter: Paternoster Press, 1978), pp. 874--902.
[7] John 14:6.
[8] Siedentop (2015), p. 360.
[9] Paul Makhuba, *Who are the Independent Churches?*

(Johannesburg: Skotaville, 1988).

[10] See for example Andrew Davison, *Amazing Love: Theology for Understanding Discipleship, Sexuality and Mission* (London: DLT, 2016), Duncan Dormor & Jeremy Morris, *An Acceptable Sacrifice? Homosexuality and the Church* (London: SPCK, 2007, Gareth Moore OP, *A Question of Truth: Christianity and Homosexuality* (London: Continuum, 2003), Adrian Thatcher, *God, Sex and Gender: An Introduction* (Chichester:Wiley-Blackwell, 2011) and Michael Vasey, *Strangers and Friends: A New Exploration of Homosexuality and the Bible* (London; Hodder and Stoughton, 1995). More conservative writers include Andrew Goddard *Homosexuality and the Church of England* (Cambridge: Grove Booklets, 2004), Peter Walker and Goddard, Andrew, *True Union in the Body? A Contribution to the discussion within the Anglican Communion concerning the public blessing of same-sex relationships* (Cambridge: Grove Booklets, 2003), Ephraim Radner, *Hope Among the Fragments: The Broken Church and Its Engagement of Scripture* (Grand Rapids, MI: Brazos Press, 2004) and Ephraim Radner and Philip Turner, *The Fate of Communion: The Agony of Anglicanism and the Future of a Global Church* (Cambridge UK: Eerdmans, 2006). For a revisionist discussion of Scriptural passages see Thatcher (2011), pp. 157–73.

[11] For example Romans 1 vv. 26--27 with its understanding of same-sex expression as un-natural and indicative of sinfulness, depends upon a notion of normality which is appropriate for those with opposite sex attraction engaging in same-sex activity but no longer plausible for a changed understanding of same-sex attraction which accepts after much research that there is a minority of people in society for whom same-sex attraction is natural.

[12] For Scripture as testimony see Walter Brueggemann, *Theology of the Old Testament: Testimony, Dispute, Advocacy* (Philadelphia: Fortress Press, 1997).

[13] The Church of England project: Living in Love and Faith

NOTES

(churchofengland.org) represents probably the most extensive exploration of the debate reflecting its complexity and contentiousness within the Anglican community.

[14] Long (2021), p. 73.

[15] See the Lambeth Declaration of 2015 and Pope Francis's Encyclical *Laudato Si: On Care for Our Common Home* (2015).

[16] I am grateful to Revd Dr Malcolm Brown, Director of the Mission and Public Affairs Division of the Archbishop's Council, for much of what follows.

[17] See https://www.churchofengland.org/sites/default/files/2017-11/shale-gas-and-fracking.pdf

[18] James Jones, *Jesus and the Earth* (London: SPCK, 2003).

[19] David Attenborough with Jonnie Hughes, *A Life on Our Planet: My Witness Statement and a Vision for the Future* (London: Ebury Publishing, 2020). See also Ruth Valerio, *Saying Yes to Life* (London: SPCK, 2020).

CHAPTER 9: IN PUBLIC

[1] Goodhart (2020), pp. 142–73.

[2] See for instance John Gray, *Enlightenment's Wake: Politics and Culture at the Close of the Modern Age* (Abingdon: Routledge, 1995) and *Seven Types of Atheism* (London: Penguin, 2019).

[3] See Holland (2019), Milbank (2009), O'Donovan (1996) and (2005), Siedentop (2015) and Williams (2012).

[4] Selby District Council Civic Service on 2nd September 2018 at All Saints, Sherburn in Elmet. Deut. 1:17; Rom. 12:9–13; Mark 10:35–45.

[5] Service of Prayer for those recently elected to Public Office on Wednesday 29th July 2015 in Selby Abbey. 1 Sam. 16; John 12:1–8.

[6] The story can be found in 1 Sam. 8–10.

[7] Sacks (2015).

[8] Selby District Council Civic Service on 9th July 2017 at St

ON YOUR BIKE

Wilfrid's Brayton. Deut. 24:10—22; Acts 28:1–16.

[9] John Milbank and Adrian Pabst, *The Politics of Virtue: Post Liberalism and the Human Face* (London: Rowman & Littlefield, 2016), p. 180.

[10] Deut. 24:21–2

[11] 12th June 2016 at St Peter and St Paul, Scrayingham. Ps. 8; Luke 12:22–31.

[12] Sermon given on 8th March 2015 at York Minister. Exod. 20:1—17; John 2:13–22.

[13] In Rowan Williams & Larry Elliot eds., *Crisis and Recovery: Ethics, Economics and Justice* (Basingstoke: Palgrave MacMillan, 2010), pp. 23–4.

[14] Williams and Elliot (2010), pp. 82–5.

[15] Isa. 42:6 and 49:6.

[16] John 2:19–21.

[17] O'Donovan (2005), p. 138.

[18] 1st June 2016 at St Mary, Hemingbrough reflecting on Isaiah 58:6—12; 2 Cor. 9:6–12.

[19] Economic contribution – Impact | UK Civil Society Almanac 2020 | NCVO

[20] Legal Service on 18th October at York Minster 2015. Isa. 55; Luke 1:1–4.

[21] John Sentamu, ed., *On Rock or Sand? Firm Foundations for Britain's Future* (2015), p. 223.

[22] Sacks (2015).

[23] Williams (2012), pp. 255–8.